GRAND SLAM

A story about two men discussing how
to cover the bases of life.

Dr. Samuel M. Huddleston

PRESS

Dedication

This book is dedicated to my grandbabies,
Samantha, Kaylin, Salin, Taylor, Kammy,
A.J., Royce Jr.,
Sophia, Chad II, Alijah, Aiden and the lady that
brings joy to my life EVERY DAY, their Noni my bride
Linda Gail.

What are others saying about Grand Slam?

"A must read with massive power for all wanting to make a positive difference with their lives. Sam Huddleston does it again with his latest book, *Grand Slam*, as his autobiography, *Five to Life*, gives great emphasis on not being trapped by one's past, his latest contribution to us all puts a finer point on it never being too late to contribute to others, community, God and self in exciting ways! - Claude E. Finn, Retired Warden, California Dept. of Corrections and Rehabilitation, (CDCR) Deuel Vocational Institution. Currently, Deputy Commissioner, Board of Prison Terms, CDCR, Retired Annuitant.

"*Grand Slam*, is a book that guides the guilt-ridden, shamed & devalued child of God back into the loving and trusting relationship God has designated for us all. Sam shows us that with Christ we come from the pit on a path that leads to the palace."
- Harry Swayne, Assistant Director of Player Programs, Baltimore Ravens; former Chaplain to the Chicago Bears, three-time NFL Champions

"Whenever I meet people who know Dr. Samuel Huddleston they immediately break forth with an enthusiastic smile and strong words of affirmation about the man who has left his signature impact on their lives. This book will impact you in much the same way."
- Doug Tawlks, M.A., Author and University Professor

"Sam Huddleston has earned the right to speak on life strategies. His life is a miracle and his book will be a blessing to many."
-Mark Rutland, Ph.D., President, ORU, Tulsa, Oklahoma

"Dr. Samuel Huddleston hits it out of the park with the content of this book. Grand Slam is extremely fundamental in its truths and should be a perennial read by both parents and young adults. Parents along with their children can and will glean much insight into life's struggles with these pillars of principle. This is a must read to avoid life's pitfalls. Dr. Huddleston outlines the basics for success in stepping to the plate in confronting life's issues verses waiting on deck while allowing life's issues to confront them."
-Jerry Manuel, 2000 Major League Manager of the Year

TABLE OF CONTENTS

Acknowledgements

This book began a long time ago as a speech I would give when speaking to students in a local Jr. High School while working with youth in Vallejo, California. After hearing someone else attempt to motivate them by using curse words, I felt then and still do today believe students can be motivated, inspired, challenged and encouraged without the curse words. Through the years there have been many individuals that have helped me in so many different ways. I must name a few of those individuals knowing I will miss some hoping they will forgive me:

Abigail Ortiz-Miller, Charla Blair, (my Administrative Assistant the last 6 years who is also a great critic and a great writer herself and one day I will be known as the man who used to work for her) Michael & Yvonne Jones and all the Jones, Ronald F. Owens Jr. (he actually took the train ride and gathered most of the factual information), Michelle Karns (an incredible lady and inspiration too many I am just one), the thousands of students who allow me to speak to them and ask the question, is this in a book... it is now. My nieces and nephews who had to listen to me tell this story over and over and over again. My grandbabies and their parents, mama, dad and daddy, my friends at Lighthouse as well as Match Two Outreach, Calandra Warren you are a gift to me. My bride Linda who not only continues to believe in me, but keeps pushing me to write. And the one who has always been there through it all without whom I have no life, Jesus the Christ the one I have followed for over 37 years. Here is my attempt to say something to the already voluminous number of books to help someone in a way that others have helped me along my life's journey. If one person is helped then all the effort was worth it. In fact one person has been helped...me, maybe you will be number two.

PREFACE

From the time I met the mysterious Poncho on a train, I knew someday I would write about the time we spent together on a brief commuter trip from Sacramento to the Bay area. When a close friend who is also a writer asked about the audience for this book, I answered, "troubled or disconnected souls." She glibly remarked that she was glad I had a specific audience in mind.

As she shook her head and looked at me, I knew she thought *I* might be troubled and disconnected— from reality. How could I possibly reach out to all those who were soul searching and disconnected? By then I had already decided that Poncho's story might just be the guide to accomplish that humungous task. Putting our dialogue down on paper brought the experience full circle. In doing so, I was finishing what needed to be done in order to reach those who have failed to develop a relationship with their families, friends and God. Troubled souls are my mission.

First of all, it is important to understand the concept of "troubled souls." We can blame it on the ties we share with the biblical Adam and Eve, but essentially people are troubled because they are human and often experience conflicts with other humans. We are all potential victims, equally frail under the laws of our humanity; the evidence of our frailty is our angst and confusion. The very nature of a "troubled" or "disconnected" soul reflects the difficulty and pain and anger of feeling hurt, frightened, uncertain, or disabled. When we lose control, we become uncertain and are prone to feel stuck. This sense of immobility provides fertile ground for self-deprecation and rampant rationalizing, which feeds decisions that further cause trouble and more emotional overload.

Emotional overloads too often create what I refer to as "disconnectedness." The weight of our problems or difficulties becomes so heavy that it breaks the positive connections we have in place to support us. It is as if we become so focused on keeping things together that we fail to keep anything working well. Chronic pain increases, causing relational discord or disconnectedness to abound, and it makes messes. Metaphorically, it is like plate spinners or jugglers – timing is everything. Without it, everything falls apart and breaks.

It is the same thing when people disconnect. They start to lose the most important things in our lives – hopes, dreams, positive beliefs about themselves, their purposes, and love between people – the relational experiences that make hearts dance.

Troubled or disconnected souls forget their relationship with God and grapple with trying to live life alone. Bad choices are the hallmark of this frame of mind; consequently, many believers become victims of their thoughts or poor decisions.

If you have ever awakened wondering why you were born, if anyone cared, or how your life had become such a mess, this book might be helpful to you. If you know a drug addict – someone who has given up a family, a job, or a lifelong passion to continue using alcohol or any other drugs— then you know a disconnected and troubled soul. Perhaps you know a parent that struggles to do his or her job. Maybe you have intentionally hurt someone or been jealous because of ghosts in your past relationship. If so, then you too might find this book helpful. Perhaps you are fearful of someone unmasking the real you, yet you secretly hope and want to be caught. Or maybe the police have real business with you because you've violated others' rights by taking their property, abusing their bodies, or manipulating their money. You might have a reason for taking some time to read this book.

It doesn't matter what your scenario is – divorce, money problems, abusive relationships, promiscuity, violence either in thought or deed, persistent fear or chronic uncertainty. What does matter is what it is doing to you. Are you lying, cheating and manipulating to get through daily life? Are you living contrary to your core beliefs? Have you lost your connection to family, friends, yourself and God?

Have you become a disconnected soul? Then my friend, you should read this book.

I have been lost. I have been disconnected and misdirected as I traveled on this earth. I have even been attracted to the dark and rowdy side of life, but I always had someone call, or better yet, *pray* me out of those places. When I was young it was my mom and dad. If they weren't physically with me, they were at the bottom of every glass or at the end of every joint. They would suddenly become present when my father's favorite song would play on the radio or whenever I saw a Bible. Remembering my mom and especially my dad always puts me in a position of having to choose between the dark and the light. Choosing *right* (or light) is not an innate human characteristic. You have to make a conscious choice to live among those who choose to accept the life that is yours for the asking. Choosing is not easy; following others is much easier.

It is said that in ancient Rome, roads were laid down on the pathways made by the livestock. However, I doubt that the livestock looked up at a hill and said, "I choose to walk over that hill to get to the other side more quickly." No. Those cows and sheep intuitively ambled along looking for water and food. They had no choice. As a result, some of the earliest Roman roads took forever to get anywhere – because cows and sheep just did not care.

Unlike those animals, people care about the roads they take. Eventually I determined, by listening to my family members and friends, where I wanted to go. I found my way to the light through the grace of God and the benevolent prayers of many good people. Now I am living a life shaped by my choices, but open to God's will.

I believe that people often cross my path so that I can hear, see and do what is right. Ordinary people in ordinary circumstances have become some of my most trusted guides to understanding the complex issues of relationships and unconditional love; they have also explained the messages in the Bible. I once knew a Skid Row man in an Alcoholics Anonymous program who told me I would find the greatest power in personal powerlessness. He said those times of crisis in my life would be when I would come closest to Christ and his agony on the cross. "Forgive them, Father" Christ said, not "SAVE ME, FATHER!" My skid row friend might as well have hit me over the head – in that moment I saw clearly that letting go of my anger that was being fed by my pain and letting God come into my life would be the choice for me. I never saw that man attend that particular group again. No one knew him or where he came from before he showed up at our meeting. I often think about how he provided just what I needed when I needed it. God answered my prayer. Sometimes that is how it happens.

This book is about another one of those ordinary people who gave me the extra-ordinary gift of new insight. Poncho helped me see how blessed I really am; the conditions of my thinking changed, and I became a different person because of a brief encounter on a train.

Please know that there is no magic or divine mysticism in this story. Although I have always hoped to have a burning bush delivered to me or receive a bolt of lightening along with a couple of stone tablets, Poncho's message came simply, but just as powerfully. In many ways I did not realize the gift he gave until he was gone.

I tell this story hoping that you too can find the wisdom to walk the path God has just for you and chose a right relationship with him through Christ, with the promise of experiencing a taste of heaven ...here on earth.

CHAPTER ONE

The Train Ride

It was a mundane Monday. I was taking the Capitol Corridor train from Sacramento to my son's home in Emeryville. I could easily make the trip faster by car, but I have always been enamored with trains. Any chance to ride on a train was a good choice in my book. It was as if I were still six years old, holding my father's hand on the platform while waiting to watch the trains come in and out of the station. I never got to ride in those days. I just imagined the freedom of riding.

It was a rare pleasure to get two hours by myself, and I was determined to turn my phone off. My office would not be able to reach me. I would be free of work.

I had a plan. The baseball stats were calling me – I had no idea what was happening in the league, but the Series was weeks away. I fantasized that I would drink too much coffee and eat junk food. I felt as though being on the train gave me dispensation from the doom and gloom of my cholesterol reading and physical last month. Furthermore, my wife, who had recently become a strict vegan, was still tempted by the barbecue ribs and hotlinks that I loved; all that great, fatty carnivore food was eliminated from my diet to support her new lifestyle. Today, however, I was thinking that I might be able to have one hotdog— just one— on the train. I was set: a train ride, some private time, a little baseball, and a hotdog meant this would be a good time, and the entire trip would culminate in hugs from my granddaughter, Samantha, and time with my handsome son, Andre. It was going to be a very good day. I remembered to thank God for all of my blessings and set about to make the day come to life.

I pushed through the double brass doors at Sacramento's I Street Train Station. There was a mural on the east wall. At first it caught my eye because of its bright colors; then I was struck by the graphic itself. Entitled, "Breaking Ground at Sacramento on January 6, 1863 for First Transcontinental Railroad," I realized I was staring at an image of our history, into a time that changed people's lives forever. Trains replaced horses and wagons, but they had also opened up the world.

While I was daydreaming about the power of technology and the technical advances of the 20th century, others around me were getting caught up in a young Latino couple's argument. It was loud, volatile and verbally abusive. She was more aggressive, but he was not totally apathetic. He gave it back; he was just not as vicious or as loud. He seemed embarrassed, too, and she seemed completely unaware that we, her audience, found her behavior inappropriate. Like many other observers, I was watching the emotional outburst between the two, though I could not figure out what caused the problem. Suddenly, he turned away from her and bumped into me with the force of a train going uphill. I had to steady myself so that I wouldn't fall. As he shook his head and smiled apologetically, he uttered, "Sorry man," under his breath.

I smiled back. I think I said it was okay. I was about to ask if there was anything I could do when we were interrupted by another outburst from his girlfriend, "Hurry UP!" she bellowed. She spoke as if he could not hear and we were not there. I found it curious that she was so out of touch with those of us who surrounded their troubled interaction. She continued with the tirade, "We're going to be late. I told you we would be late. We'll miss the train. I told you we should have left earlier so I could get a good seat."

I was amazed. All this was for a good seat on a train that no one was boarding yet? I must have looked perplexed because the young man looked at me as he shrugged his shoulders and brandished another grim smile. I smiled too. I wanted to say something, but I wasn't sure what would be appropriate. I watched him trail after her and realized that I wanted to save him from the scorn and ridicule he was suffering. As her scowling and cursing continued, the couple proceeded through the terminal and exited through the other set of brass doors that led to the waiting train on Track 4.

I followed them. Looking at the mural for the last time, I exited through the brass doors and hurried to catch the same train. We were going to share a ride.

I had already decided to take a seat as far away from others as possible. I needed one of those little tables in front of me. Finding a perfect spot, I laid out all kinds of work materials and my laptop to look as though I intended to be quite busy. It was camouflage to deter others from sitting anywhere near me. I put on my "I am way too personally reflecting" face so that no one would talk to me. As I started to relax, Andre and Samantha came to mind. We were going to have fun on this visit. I always like being with my grandchildren.

The young couple was ahead of me in the car. They were still loudly bickering. These two didn't seem to mind calling attention to themselves and their problems. Other folks were blatantly staring and trying to avoid the couple at the same time.

The train was not crowded. There were plenty of seats. Many people were shaking their heads as they moved away from the couple; they left the train car so they would not be disturbed, yet somehow I got it in my head that I should move closer to them. Perhaps they might need to talk. Maybe those half smiles from the young man were a call for some kind of a connection. I knew I was giving up My Plan — baseball stats, privacy, hotdogs, and quiet time—but perhaps I was trading it in for HIS Plan.

My rule is to never question HIS Plan, but just to do what is in front of me. This couple had been screaming for attention for nearly half an hour. We were finally seated. The train jerked forward and the journey began. I opened my briefcase and started riffling through my papers. Frankly, I was reflecting on my decision to sit and wait to be needed by this couple. Was I being presumptuous? Was this HIS will or was I being nosy?

Before long I was called out of my reverie. *She* wanted a pad and paper. He had neither. She complained. He looked to me for help, and I was able to oblige. I gave him a yellow legal pad. "Take all you need," I said. He quickly tore off a few pages and handed it back to me across the aisle. He looked me straight in the eye and asked, "Hey, man, what's your name?"

"My name is Sam," I responded.

"I'm Poncho."

We were on our way until Poncho's girlfriend noticed that she didn't have his attention.

"Shut up, Poncho. What are you talking to him for? Is he your lover?"

I'll never forget what happened next. Poncho jumped up and yelled, "SHUT UP!" in a tone equal to the ugliness she had been incessantly spewing. She grabbed his jersey, but he pulled away. Enraged, she resumed her cursing and then stormed away down the aisle. In an obvious attempt to avoid being humiliated in front of me, Poncho yelled back, "You shut up, woman. The man gave me some paper! Maybe he can help us!" But by this time, the woman was so far down the aisle she couldn't have heard him.

I watched the woman stomp off away from us. I bet she was thinking to herself, *"He should come after me when I walk away. I don't like the looks of that black dude with him – he looks dangerous – all dressed up like some kinda salesman. God only knows what he'll get into on his own...he really is a loser. I can't stand how we have to live and everything falls on me. If he didn't have me, he wouldn't have anyone. Where is he? What could he possibly have to talk about with that stranger?"*

Poncho looked back at me, hung his head in embarrassment, and shrugged. He sat across from me and stared out the window. A few moments of awkward silence passed as the train eased out of the station.

We crossed the Sacramento River and headed west. I remembered the mural and uttered a quick word of thanks that I didn't have to ride a wagon train. I doubt anything like this happened when people were traveling in wagon trains. I wondered when it became okay to curse, scream and be so disrespectful in public.

Out of the corner of my eye, I noticed Poncho was looking at me. I was nicely dressed in a tailored suit and Italian leather shoes, and he appeared to be wondering what kind of guy I was. Finally he broke the ice. His first question was about what I did for a living.

"You're dressed really nice. What do you do?"

"I work for an international organization that searches for lost people."

"Say what? Do you mean like those kids on the milk cartons?"

I hesitated for a moment.

"No, I am not part of the search for exploited or lost children that are on the milk cartons." I could tell he was under the influence of more than just the soft drink in his hand, and his face registered a quizzical look as he asked me to repeat myself.

"An international organization that searches for lost people."

He was not intimidated. He asked for more information about searching for people.

I leaned back and looked straight into his blood-shot brown eyes, I could tell he was tired, but it wasn't just from lack of sleep; it was from living. I could tell he was lost—disconnected, too. "Poncho, what we do is travel around the country searching for people who have been disconnected from their families, from other important relationships in their lives, even from themselves." I wanted to get into a discussion about why becoming disconnected is so dangerous – disconnected people seldom have the will to live their lives according to what is "right." They become dangerous to all of us, but most of all they are dangerous to themselves and the people who love and lose them.

Poncho had an agenda. He was in charge of this conversation.

"And what do you do when you find them?" Poncho asked suspiciously. "Do you put 'em somewhere?"

"We try to get them reconnected." I wasn't sure that he was getting the "reconnected" piece. As I tried to explain he asked another question.

"Yeah? How do you do that?"

"Well, we talk with people and as we work with them, we try to step into the their life experiences by asking questions and listening carefully. It usually doesn't take long before we can tell in what way they're disconnected. If we find out the problem is alcohol, we connect them with an organization that can help them, like Alcoholics Anonymous."

"Oh. Well, what if they're on drugs?" He dropped his eyes then looked out the window as the train began to accelerate and gently rock back and forth.

"Well, if they're on drugs we try to get them connected to an organization like Narcotics Anonymous or Teen Challenge. If we sense that they are disconnected in their relationships, we direct them to a counselor. Do you know where we find people are the most disconnected?"

"No, where?" he inquired.

"In love, but what they don't realize is that the love they are missing isn't from a girlfriend or boyfriend. It's an unconditional kind of love that comes from having a relationship with God. Ultimately, the people we search for are spiritually disconnected."

Poncho looked curious. His breathing was shallow. I waited for him to say something, but he just looked at me with ever-saddening eyes. I continued.

"We've found that people get into trouble when they are separated from God and their <u>beliefs in goodness</u>. For many people, drinking, using other drugs, abusing others, or feeling overwhelmed with life starts when they are disconnected from God's grace or an understanding that they will be okay. It's easy to make bad choices when you feel like no one will notice or care."

I went on to explain that this organization I work with tries to reconnect people with God first. I told him, "We have found that many times when people get reconnected with God, they are able to deal with the other issues in their lives. It is almost as if they have to know that they are cared about and connected to do what is right for their lives. We try to create the conditions in which troubled people can make good decisions to turn around their lives with the care and support of a non-threatening, non-judgmental guide who can help provide on-ramps to a relationship with God, a loving father."

"Amazing. What's your success rate?"

"For people who listen to what we say and who follow the counsel we give, the success rate is 100 percent."

"Wait – you're telling me that anyone who just does what you tell them gets, uh, reconnected somehow to God and all the other people in his life?"

"That is exactly what I am saying."

As I spoke, I began to realize I unwaveringly believe that a relationship with God fixes the broken and heals the wounded. It occurred to me that I was not just telling Poncho about my job; I was telling him about *my* life. I wondered if he was helping me or if I was helping him.

"I'm telling you – no, I can promise you, Poncho: Bring God into your life and it will change forever. I don't mean that the pain and struggles or nasty people all go away. I mean you'll handle things differently, from a position of grace, rather than from a position of anger or distress. If you'll let me, I'll share with you the five principles we use to get people on that road to reconnection. Is that okay with you?"

"Yeah, I guess, " he answered. I could see that he was wondering why he had ever spoken to me, while I was thanking God for delivering him. I took a deep breath, and jumped in.

"Hand me one of those sheets of paper I gave you, would you?"

I invited Poncho to sit next to me so he wouldn't have to look at my writing upside down. Since his girlfriend hadn't returned, he agreed to move over. Oblivious to the people around us, I started right in.

"Poncho, I'm going to show you five principles. If you begin to apply what I'm going to tell you, I guarantee your life will change and you'll never be the same again."

"Guarantee? You can guarantee something like that?"

"I guarantee it!" I said.

I wrote the letters B-A-S-E-S vertically on the left margin of the legal pad and drew a baseball diamond. "This, Poncho, is what we call an acronym. Maybe you've heard of those."

"Yeah, sounds familiar from school, but I don't remember anything about it."

"An acronym is just a word formed from the first letters of other words. In this case, the B stands for 'Banish Blame.' I wrote it on the pad. "The first thing you have to do is stop blaming others for your mistakes or your situation." I continued writing. "Next we have A, which stands for 'Accept Responsibility.' In this step you begin to take responsibility for your own actions. The first S stands for 'Seek Help,' which is a real challenge, especially for men. Then we have E, which stands for 'Envision Success.' This one can be difficult, too. And the final S stands for 'Structure a Step-by-Step Plan.' You must have a plan in life to help you get where you want to go."

"So, man, how did you figure all this out?" Poncho wondered aloud.

"Years ago, in prison."

"You? You were locked up?"

"Yep, me. And prison is the place where I found freedom."

"But I don't understand. How can you be free while you're locked up? It doesn't make sense."

"My life turned around in prison, Poncho. It's where I learned many of the things I'm sharing with you now."

He dropped his head, then turned to his left and stared out the window again. We were still moving, but Poncho didn't seem to notice the passing landscape. He seemed to be looking way beyond the scenery. Perhaps he was thinking, *"I like this Sam guy. He seems for real believing all that God stuff. Like God came and told him the secrets of the universe... At least he's not preachy ... but he seems so happy. I haven't felt this good in a conversation in years. My old lady thinks I am useless and treats me like I haven't had a thought since Jesus was a baby. Dang... I know that leaving her on this train by herself its gonna cost me. But I want to hear what the dude has to say... I'm doing this for me."*

"Poncho, I don't want you to make the same mistakes I made."

"Me neither," he mumbled. "I guess that's why I'm still listening."

I have to admit that I smiled at his admission. He was listening, hoping that I had something to say that would make a difference, and I was talking, hoping to say something that would encourage him to become different. Goethe once said, *"If I accept you as you are, I could make you worse. If I treat you as if you already are what you are capable of becoming, I can help you become that."*

I wholeheartedly agree.

CHAPTER TWO

The Blame Game

So there I was, sitting somewhere between West Sacramento and Davis, riding an Amtrak train headed for Emeryville. To my left stretched the Yolo Causeway, an area designed to control flooding during the rainy season. To my right, rice fields sprinkled the flat landscape. And next to me sat Poncho, a disconnected dude who needed help. I was determined to help him find his way. I just needed to find out how and why he had been "dissed."

- Was he *Discounted?* – Was he feeling like there was no hope or relief?
- Was he *Disrespected?* – In his community, was he ever talked about positively or as an asset?
- Was he *Disconnected?* – Could old friends find him or reach out?
- Was he *Discouraged?* – Could he see his own value and worth?

- Or did his pain come from being *Disengaged?* – Had he become cynical and unwilling to reach out anymore?

Feeling "dissed" has many origins, but always the same consequences. It causes a pervasive sense of immobility that often seems permanent. Some people call it "pessimism," but it is greater than an "ism" – it is a state of mind. It feels like a heavy burden. No wonder kids in the street are so averse to being "dissed."

I had to find an opening, a way to connect. I noticed Poncho's green and white Oakland A's jersey and hat. He was definitely a baseball fan. I sensed that my BASES approach might strike a chord with him. Perhaps it would hold his attention as our conversation continued, but I needed to start with my own vulnerability. I learned long ago to never ask another to be vulnerable until I was willing to be open myself. So I went for it.

"Poncho, what kind of mistakes do you think I might have made?"

He seemed to still be considering my statement about wanting to help him avoid my mistakes. He was looking a bit defensive. I leaned back and left a bit of silence in the space between us. He finally responded, "I have no idea, what kind of mistakes do you think I've made?"

"I don't know what mistakes you've made, man, but I can tell you that it's never too late to start a new beginning. You don't want to start over – that will put you back where you have been. You have to step off one track and start a new way of being, thinking and doing. In Alcoholics Anonymous, they have a saying that goes something like, 'You can't think your way into a new way of living, but you can live your way into a new way of thinking.' Change requires action. Most people will only pay the price of change if the benefit is greater than the cost of the change and more beneficial than staying the same.

"That is why so many people fail on diets, for example. They think the price is too high and the benefit too low. Besides, they know how to be overweight. They don't necessarily know how to be thin, so they stay the same, and America has become the fattest country on the planet. A lot of overweight people would say that they aren't hurting anybody; they say it is their body and that it is nobody's business. Sound familiar?"

Poncho sat back and breathed deeply. I could tell that the baseball diamond I drew had piqued his interest. "Okay, go ahead," he said. "Tell me how that little diamond is going to get me off drugs and make everybody stay on a diet." Well, at least he was listening. I laughed out loud. I think I said something about his great sense of humor, and then I pointed to my diagram.

"In many ways, life is like the game of baseball. You know about the on deck circle, right? It's the place where the batter stands before moving up to the plate. Well, in the game of life, some batters live their whole existence 'on deck.' They never even attempt to get to the plate, and they blame others for their own unwillingness to compete."

"I'm not sure what you mean."

"Some people blame everyone else for what they are and what they've become. I tell my grandkids the story of the *Loser's Limp*. Did you learn it in school?" Poncho shook his head and said he hadn't learned much in school.

"Well," I continued, "the *Loser's Limp* is one of my favorite stories. It's simple, really. Imagine a track race — the runners all bunched together, shoulder-to-shoulder, pacing themselves but pumping hard. Suddenly one runner shoots ahead, quickly followed by a second. Both are running hard and fast. So fast they've left the pack behind. One of these athletes is going to be the winner. They're neck-in-neck. They continue to run hard, but one runner realizes that he might not make it to the finish line first. As he becomes increasingly concerned with winning, he begins to slow his pace and fall behind. Instead of shaking it off and pulling his strength together for the final lap, he decides to feign an injury. After all, no one could blame him for not winning if he was hurt. He could get out of the embarrassment of not being good enough to win. Instead of trying, he lets himself fall and pretends that he has somehow injured his leg. Needless to say, the other runner won the race.

"The *Loser's Limp* is about cowardice and blame. Some people live their whole lives limping from a fake fall, Poncho. At times, they use food, alcohol, other drugs, or anger to deal with not winning at life."

Poncho hung his head and confessed that he might have a SMALL drug and alcohol problem, but quickly added that he wasn't a bad person. It was obvious that he was really concerned that I not think he was 'a bad person.'

"At least I don't – I mean, at least I didn't sell the stuff, man. You know what I'm saying?"

His face told me all I needed to know: his substance abuse problem was not all in the past, but my place was not to judge or guess about the problem. I was there to guide him to possible solutions or different ways of thinking that might lead to new ways of being. I knew he needed to hear what he was saying.

"But Poncho, drugs are illegal. And besides, even though you might not be profiting from someone else's choice to use, you are still choosing to risk your own life, and that's not okay. You're hurting yourself."

If I had a dollar for every time I've said those words I could buy my own train. Invariably, half of the folks I've had the opportunity to speak to don't care; the other half jumped into the conversation by telling me that their drug use was not my business. I had often wondered how could I respond to their defensiveness, then one day, I realized that the best answer I could make was simply this: telling the truth.

I said to Poncho, "When I was sitting in your seat across from the man who said those words to me, I remember thinking that it was not his business. And besides, I believed I could handle what I did."

Poncho looked at me with a scowl and added, "Yeah. Yeah, what kind of a preacher does drugs?"

"I don't think drugs are your problem," I responded. "In a lot of ways they weren't my problem either. They are just a consequence of being disconnected from the life you really want to be living. Drugs have you believing that you are connected, when in reality you are investing in a lie. The more you use, the more you have to add to the lie. Some people lose touch with reality to protect their lies, but when everything crashes, with whom and to what are they hooked? I know these things because they are part of my story. My relationship with drugs nearly cost me all my important connections – to myself, to my friends and family, and most of all, to God.

"For me drugs were a cover-up for pain, yet they caused me to disconnect even more. It became a vicious cycle. I needed help to get off the drugs, but most of all I needed help to reconnect to positive and productive people and to the things which used to make me proud to be me—things like loyalty, being a hard worker, having brains and being smart. However, to reestablish these connections, I had to admit that I was no longer connected to anyone or anything, not even to the people I was with everyday. I had become empty and lost."

I asked Poncho if he was satisfied living this way or whether the on deck circle was where he wanted to stay. He failed to respond immediately; instead he stared out the window pensively. As he gazed out the window, I thought about how people who are stuck seldom see that there might be a way to become less stuck. Maybe the baseball metaphor would help to explain.

"Don't you ever want to step up to the batter's box to see what you can do?" I asked. "Don't you want to see if there is any juice inside you that will help you hit the ball when it comes over home plate?"

He bolted from the seat next to me and returned to the one across the table. After an uncomfortable moment's silence, he looked me directly in the eyes as I began to speak again. I thought I might have pushed too hard, but I had already started, and there seemed to be a reason that we met and talked. I decided to follow His lead.

With anger and disdain Poncho said, "Get out of my head, man! These things didn't happen to you."

I didn't want Poncho to shut down completely, so cautiously I asked, "May I tell you a story about something that happened years ago when I was behind bars?" He nodded his approval and I continued. "When I was in prison, I took a class taught by a man named Bob. He was an educated, successful businessman who used a lot of big words when he lectured—at least they seemed big to us. You see, the average reading level of prisoners at that time was sixth grade. Many of the guys could not understand the things Bob was saying, so they got together one day and elected me to tell him that though we appreciated his coming to the prison to teach us free of charge, we wanted him to break things down and make them more on our level.

"When Bob returned the next week, I spoke up. 'Bob,' I said, 'I've been asked to thank you for coming and teaching us each week. We know we couldn't possibly pay you enough to take time to come down here and do this for us. But man, I mean sir, most of us haven't had a lot of education, and many of us don't read very well. We don't know what all those words are that you use, and your ways of explaining things get us confused sometimes. We were wondering if you could sort of break things down into easier pieces for us. You know, to our level.' I waited.

"When he didn't respond, I sat down with all the other men around me nodding their heads in agreement. I felt pretty good about myself right about then. I was a leader."

"You said that?" Poncho asked, incredulously. "You told him he wasn't teaching right?" Poncho asked. "I bet that dude thought you—"

"Well, what could he do?" I interrupted and grinned. "I was already in prison."

Poncho laughed. "Dang, what did he do? Did he quit? Did he kick you out of the class? What did he say?"

"He asked one of the most important questions I've ever been asked. Bob lowered his glasses to the tip of his nose, glanced around the room at all of us, and then stared right at me. Slowly, and with such intensity he asked, *'Is that where you want to stay?'* The room grew deathly quiet. You won't believe what happened next. Some of the guys were so mad, they stormed out of the room."

"Yeah, well, I'm sorry, but I think I probably would have jetted, too!" Poncho admitted. "It doesn't sound like he cared much about your feelings."

"He didn't care, Poncho," I continued. "And you know what? My feelings were hurt. My first reaction was to tell him to kiss my— you know what, because he couldn't possibly understand what I had just said; I felt that if he lived where I had, then he might be able to talk to me like he was my daddy. But, what he said made me reflect because I think my father would have said something just like that.

"But man, I wanted to leave! I felt like what he said was rude and insensitive. I felt truly dissed. but I didn't leave; there would be no loser's limp for me. For what might have been the first time in my life, something about what he said made me determined to prove he wasn't going to beat me. I was gonna make it in his class. Instead of tuning out whenever he used a word or a term I didn't understand, I wrote it down, went back to my dorm, and looked it up in my dictionary. Then I memorized that definition and made a point to use it in a sentence when I spoke with him the next week in class. I became a regular vocabulary nerd.

"I don't think he ever knew what I was doing or how his question had affected me. My internal answer was 'Hell, no, I don't want to stay where I am!' That wasn't where I wanted to stay—physically, mentally, emotionally or spiritually. You see, Poncho, I was disconnected from myself, my family, God, and society; but I was beginning to be aware of just how far away I was from where I wanted to be."

"To this day, I often ask myself, 'Is that where you want to stay?' So many things make it easy to stay the same. Sometimes people say they don't want us to change. They claim they'll love us anyway. It's tempting just to stay right where we are because it feels safe and warm, and because staying the same demands nothing from us. In the end, though, it means sacrificing our drive and zeal for life.

Poncho leaned back and stared out the window. The train was rolling into Davis Station, and students from the university were pouring in with their backpacks and laptops. Even though they were nestled in their own little worlds via cell phones and iPods, they exuded a sense of purpose, evidence that their lives were moving forward, thanks to more than just a train ride.

Poncho's body language began to change. He was a bit older than the incoming flux of students, and he felt the need to exhibit his street bravado in order to impress them. I doubt they noticed; I pretended not to.

"Say, Poncho, you want something to drink?" I asked.

"No, man, I'm good. Go ahead with your story."

"Years ago I used to play baseball. I'm betting you've played some baseball, too. Am I right?"

Poncho's face lit up. "Sure did!" he said. "I was pretty good at it, too!"

"Well, you know then that baseball is like most other sports; the purpose is to score points, except in baseball, it's runs you're after. You step out of the dugout and into the on deck circle where you wait your turn to go up to bat, hoping for your chance to earn a run for your team. But you don't just stand still. A good player will practice swinging the bat. He'll also use that time to study how the pitcher is throwing the ball to the batter ahead of him. If the batter in front of you gets on base, you have a responsibility to contribute to that success. Everything and everyone is connected. It's through our relationships that we learn how to live our lives, but most of all, our relationships help us define who we are in the world."

"Yeah, Sam, I was good at that part. That's sort of the game within the game," Poncho added.

"Then you know what I'm talking about. When it's your turn at the plate, you hope to hit the ball and get to first base. Your next goal is to get to second base, then third, and then home to score a run. Well, life is kind of like that. Each time you reach home, you are closer to becoming the person you were designed to be, reconnected to life and ful-filling your destiny.

"But what happens if you don't know the rules of the game? What if you've never played baseball? What if you came to play, but you weren't ready? Then what do you do? Let me give you an example of what I mean."

I shared with Poncho how I coached my eight-year-old son's baseball team years ago. I was a full-time college student and working part-time at night, but Royce, my oldest son, had sort of "volunteered" me to be the coach. This was his first time playing an organized sport, and to my surprise, none of the other kids had played on a team before, either, so taking on this project was a bigger challenge than it looked.

Poncho said, "Wow, Sam. My dad was never interested enough in me to even take me to a game. No one ever came to anything I did at school."

"That must have been tough" I said, noting the faraway look of hurt in his eyes. I was reminded of my need to be grateful for all that my father did for me, even though he stayed way too busy with work.

Poncho continued, "Yeah. It still bugs me that I never could please him. I don't even think he knows who I am or what I am about. I just stay away."

Despite his thinly veiled efforts to conceal his hurt, he was beginning to open up. I glanced at my watch and quickly calculated about how much longer we had on the train, trying to make sure I would have enough time to share all the principles of the BASES with Poncho. However, I veered from the subject just long enough to share a bit about being raised with five siblings in a broken home. My father cared, but often he was working so hard that he had no time for the things I longed to do with him.

"Anyway," I said, "there I was at our first practice. I had a whistle in my mouth, a clipboard in my hand, and a sharpened No. 2 pencil behind my ear. From my roster on the clipboard, I called out each player's name. As each one yelled, 'Here!' I asked, 'What position do you want to play?' Most of them responded, 'I don't care, Coach. I just want to play!'

"I assigned each of them one of the bases or field positions, but soon my son interrupted me, saying, 'Dad, none of the guys are where you told them to go.' I looked up from my roster, and sure enough, they were all in center field. They were throwing up invisible balls and making some great catches! I guess you could say they were all wrapped up in playing their own version of baseball. I watched them for a few moments, then blew my whistle and called them back to home plate.

"After watching them, I devised a plan. As they gathered around, I said 'All right!' On the count of three, I want each of you to run the bases. Start at first, then run to second, then third, and finally home. Okay— one, two, three, GO!' I didn't point out where the bases were or tell them in which direction to run. I wanted to see if they knew.

"Poncho, you wouldn't have believed it. One of the kids ran straight past first base toward the fence. Another ran to third base. One boy ran straight to second, and another ran to the pitcher's mound. They didn't have the first idea how to 'cover the bases.' Not one of them, other than my own son, knew how to run the bases to play the game. Not one."

I could tell I had Poncho's interest now. I told him how one of the boys who lived near the park ran home crying. His dad brought him back and angrily confronted me. He demanded to know if I sent his son home because he wasn't good enough for my team. I told him that I had instructed the players to run the bases and come home, not *go* home!

The father looked at me, then to his son. He smiled at me and said something under his breath that sounded a lot like "good luck!"

Poncho laughed out loud. His face relaxed when he laughed. He seemed years younger and his eyes glistened. He told me of a time when his dad was teaching him to ride a bike. He explained it like this:

"He told me to do everything that he said. I did. When he told me to push the pedals and not worry about falling, I did it. As the bike started to move on its own with me riding, I just kept pumping away. I ran right into the back of my dad's old pick up. He screamed, 'Why didn't you stop?' as he was picking me up off the ground and checking my knees. I said, 'You didn't tell me to stop.'

'What?' he exclaimed.

'You didn't tell me to stop,' I said. He just shook his head and tried not to show me he was laughing."

I told Poncho now he could understand why I knew that it was going to be a long, hot summer. And it was. I realized that if my team was ever going to learn the game of baseball, as their coach I would have to teach them how to "cover the bases." I reminded him that life is kind of like a game of baseball. On the diagram of the baseball diamond I drew, I wrote four rules that applied to baseball and life, hoping that he'd be able to see the connection.

Rule No. 1: Regardless of what path you choose, *everything you do has consequences*. Life has lots of rules, and when you think they don't apply to you or when you choose to break them, you'll pay a high price. Some rules are pretty clear. If you don't practice the piano, then you won't be ready for the piano recital. If you steal, you could get caught. If you lie, you might have to lie again to protect your first lie. When you don't follow the rules, you always have to be on the look out for negative consequences. Make good decisions so you'll be at peace with their potential outcomes. For example, if you tell the truth, then some people might not like you. I asked Poncho, "Can you live with it?"

"I get it," he said.

Rule No. 2: If you want to be a winner, you can't go it alone. *It takes the help of the other players to win the game.* That saying, "There's no *I* in team" may be a truism, but it's true. No baseball team will ever play well without a group of individuals becoming something together that they could not have been alone: a team. Success in life also relies on an individual's ability to work with others.

To further explain, I told Poncho about my friend, the soloist, in the joint. He had an incredible voice. We all liked to listen to him, and he liked to be heard. One of our prison clergy decided that it might be a good thing to organize a "jailhouse choir." A bunch of us with pretty good voices joined. Frankly, we liked the time that was dedicated to practicing with the pastor's wife who directed our church choir, but we also like to sing. It was a surprise when James, the talented soloist, asked to participate in choir. He joined and we never got to sing together again. We tried, but James always had to harmonize or lead, even when there was no place for him. People started to drop out of the choir because it wasn't fun to sing anymore. James would yell at folks and tell them they did not have the voice for the choir.

Eventually the pastor's wife put a stop to it all. She simply told us that the role of God was already taken, and He wasn't looking for any back up singers. Nothing more was said. James became a member of the group. He was hesitant at first, but after awhile he started to appreciate being on the team – or in this case, the choir. We were quite special after that change in venue. I often still tell people (and remind myself) that the role of God is already taken, but we are needed to be part of the support team.

Poncho looked at me like my wife sometimes does. He seemed to be saying, "Are you for real?" I tried to pre-empt his question by saying, "I do love to tell about what has happened to me. I constantly find that other people have had the same kinds of experiences. When we connect with each other's stories, we get closer in our relationships. For example, someday you will tell this story about being on the train with a squared-off dude in well-tailored clothes who told good stories. Right?"

Poncho let out a big, loud laugh. "You're right. I'm already wondering why I started to talk to you."

"There are never any accidents, Poncho. We were meant to meet each other. I, too, wonder why we connected. I just trust you are here to teach me something."

"You think I am going to teach you?" Poncho asked astonished.

"Yep. You already have. Let me give you the rest of the life rules. Then we'll have more to talk about. The next rule, for example, is hard for a lot of people to grapple with because it has to do with fairness."

Rule No. 3: *Life isn't fair*, and sometimes you won't like the calls. But it's how you respond to the calls, even the ones that aren't fair, that will determine your success in life. Remember when you played baseball, and you just knew the umpire was blind because he couldn't possibly have seen that the ball was clearly out of the strike zone? Or when you knew your runner was safe, but the ump called him out? Did you get your way? No, you had to accept the umpire's call whether you thought it was right or not. It's the same thing in life. Sometimes things just aren't fair.

I asked Poncho if he knew who Arthur Ashe was. He thought for a moment and said "No, not really." I told him that Arthur Ashe was a famous professional tennis player who had competed against and beaten some of the best tennis players in history. He was the first African American player ever to win the men's singles at Wimbledon, the most prestigious tennis tournament in the world.

As a world-class athlete, Mr. Ashe had taken very good care of himself and seemed to be very healthy, but when he was only 46 years old he had a major heart attack and had to have coronary bypass surgery to save his life. The surgery was a success, and though he had to give up tennis, he expected to live a long and healthy life. Then, in 1988 Arthur Ashe was told that he had contracted HIV, a deadly virus that wasn't even very well understood in those years, as a result of a blood transfusion during surgery. Most people acquire HIV because they share dirty needles or they abuse their bodies in other ways, but not Arthur Ashe! Physically, he had done all the right things. But in 1993 he died from complications of AIDS, the disease caused by HIV.[1] When Arthur Ashe died, he left behind a beautiful wife and a six-year-old daughter. You see, my young friend: life isn't fair."

"That's sad, real sad." Poncho said.

"Yes it is, but Mr. Ashe didn't expect life to be fair. One day, when one of his fans asked him why God had chosen him to get such a bad disease, he answered,

The world over, 50 million children start playing tennis. 5 million learn to play tennis, 500,000 learn professional tennis, 50,000 come to the circuit, 5,000 reach the grand slam, 50 reach Wimbledon, four to the semifinals, two to the finals. When I was holding a (victory) cup I never asked God, 'Why me?'[2] And today, in pain, I should not be asking God, 'Why me?'

You see, Arthur Ashe knew that life isn't always fair, and that, despite his illness, he had still been blessed."

"Sounds like a hard lesson," Poncho said. "Are there any more of your rules for life?"

"Yes," I answered. "There's one more, and it's a very serious one."

Rule No. 4: *When you don't play by the rules, you can get hurt*, but even when you play by all the rules, you can still get hurt. You can face disappointment, and you may experience tragedy. I turned the paper around and pointed it in Poncho's direction. As he studied the four rules I had written out, I reflected on the current state of our country.

"How completely we have devolved from 'In God We Trust' to the 'Me Generation' that demands rights without responsibilities," I mused. "Significant but subtle changes – the increasing divorce rate, a decline in general moral values, hypnotic music that glorifies abuse, illicit sex and illegal drugs – all these things provide escape and temporary pleasure for people who don't know how to or don't want to learn how to handle their emotional pain. Our country is at a crossroads. We must look beyond drugs, guns, welfare, movies, racism, single mothers and absent fathers. These are all just symptoms of deeper problems."

I challenged Poncho. "Life," I said, "is about learning to deal with inevitable pain, and moving forward at the same time, even if the pain doesn't go away. It's tempting to find someone to blame when the tough times come. And they will come. But it's not about placing blame." Revisiting my baseball metaphor, I invited him to examine how the power that we give blame keeps us from moving forward in life. "Blame is when you point your finger at someone or something else as the cause of your failure to score. It's saying that someone else is responsible. It's giving the umpire, the coach, the other team, or the rowdy fans the power to paralyze you and keep you from becoming a winner."

"Yeah, Sam," Poncho offered. "I see what you mean, but I know I'm the way I am because people messed me up. I mean, I'm not going to totally blame them and all, but I am a product of my environment, right?"

"Poncho, people may have mistreated you, and caused you pain, but you still have to take responsibility for your own actions and for how you've responded to their mistreatment. I didn't get sent to prison because my parents divorced; I went to prison for acting out my anger and the pain it caused me."

The train had left the Davis station and was headed down the track for the next 25-minute portion of the ride. Passengers made their way back and forth to the Café Car, and the conductor slowly worked his way up the aisle collecting tickets. All of a sudden, Poncho panicked.

"Aw, man, where's my ticket?" he said, fumbling through his backpack. "Oh no, I wonder if my old lady has it?" He rummaged frantically through all his pockets and belongings.

"Found it!" he said, just in time to present it to the slightly amused conductor.

We continued our talk, returning to the theme of the on deck circle. I said to him, "Fear of getting hurt keeps a lot of people from moving on. When they do get hurt, they keep themselves frozen in place, afraid to try again, but these rules can change a person's life. If I had learned these principles when I was your age, I would have made different choices; I wouldn't have broken my parents' hearts and hurt a lot of innocent people."

I glanced at my watch and realized we only had about an hour-and-a-half more on the train, and we still had a lot of material to cover. I told Poncho I wanted to go over some principles with him.

"Principles?" Poncho asked.

"Well," I said, with a slight chuckle, "principles are personal laws that help an individual overcome the habits and obstacles that keep him or her from being the very best he or she can be." I mentioned them briefly a moment ago.

"Oh, okay. Go for it. What are they? I forgot what you said. Can you teach me?"

"I can try. I have had to learn and relearn them, so we can talk about them together. First we've got to Banish Blame. Next we must Accept Responsibility and Seek Help. Finally, we should Envision Success and Structure a Step-by-Step Plan for achieving our goals. It's the way I make sure I get to run around all of life's BASES."

Poncho grew silent as he thought about my principles. Breaking the silence, I ventured, "Everyone has a different way to use these principles. My friends who are recovering alcoholics don't go to bars, or hang with people who drink too much. What principle is that linked to from BASES?"

Poncho answered quickly: "A, 'Accept RESPONSIBILITY.' "

He continued, "What about the poor kid whose parents left him. Now he is a thief because he never had what other kids had? He's on 'B' for 'Banish BLAME.' "

Poncho had really been listening. We played the "Which of the BASES am I on if...?" game for another ten minutes, and each time Poncho chose the right principle. He could even back up his decision. I was impressed with his perception and candor.

I looked at my watch and thought I had just enough time to bring this all "home." "All right," I went on, "you're up to bat next. The player ahead of you is trying his best to get on a base. The person behind you has to wait for you. From the on deck circle you can see the entire game as you wait your turn, and in that moment, you know that all eyes will focus on you as you attempt to get on base." I pointed out that in life, many people never leave the on deck circle. They either don't want to take part in it, or they're afraid that if they step up to the plate, they might strike out or make some foolish mistake. So they stay where they are and make excuses instead of trying for a hit.

I asked Poncho if he knew the most common excuse people use. He ventured a guess, "It's not my fault?" The corners of his mouth spread into a slight grin. He understood exactly where this was going.

"That's right, my friend. Many people excuse their behavior by placing responsibility somewhere else. They feel somebody, something, some situation made them do it. They say things like, 'It's the drugs, it's the government, it's my race. I'm a girl, I'm a boy, I'm too young, I'm too old. I was raised by a single mother. My father was never home. I've got a handicap.' And what are the results of feeling and living like a victim? Suicides, murders, alcohol abuse and drug overdoses, sexual crimes, physical and emotional abuse. And more blame.

"All of us have been through situations and circumstances that have 'disabled' us; we all have problems. Some 'disabilities' are more visible than others and some seem more tragic, but nothing has happened to you that hasn't also happened to many others who chose to move beyond their circumstances rather than use them as excuses."

"So what's your point, man? This is one messed up world."

"My point is that society is filled with young people who have unwillingly been victimized because they suffered at the hands of someone else. Now, by choice, they have stayed victims. Sure, you can go on living this way, but if you truly want to win in life, you can't go on blaming others. People do terrible things to one another, but your response is your responsibility, Poncho. No one can make you do anything you don't want to do."

I reminded Poncho of Bob and how he had asked me, "Is that where you want to stay?"

After all these years, I still ask myself that question. Why? Like every other human, I'm still tempted to blame other people for my shortcomings. I was living my life as a victim. I blamed God, my mother and father, white folks, the police, Asians, black folks, my teachers — everybody and everything I could think of. I pointed the finger everywhere but at myself for my problems as a rebellious, runaway, drug-crazed teenager. I felt that society was to blame for my going to prison. I knew if everyone treated me right, then I'd be just as successful as the next guy.

But one day I had sort of a revelation. It finally dawned on me that even if I couldn't change my environment or my circumstances, *I could change me.* Only I could walk through the pain of my past hurt so I wouldn't remain paralyzed in the present or the future. In my heart I was answering Bob's question: No, I didn't want to stay here, but in order to move, I had to admit that my own choices were keeping me a victim.

"Poncho," I said, "lots of people like me have been released from prison and have made something of their lives. Others have overcome racial and gender discrimination and risen to the top of their chosen fields. Women have escaped abusive situations or recovered from the horrendous crime of rape and have learned to trust again. Accident and combat victims have overcome seemingly insurmountable handicaps to get back in the game. Some people beat the odds when they choose to live differently. Notice that I said when they CHOOSE to make that difference. They decide that nothing – a bad prognosis, chronic problems, or the current circumstance – would keep them disconnected from life. It's not easy, but people make the choices every day that transform them from victims into victors.

"I have a friend, Rev. Gary Hoyt, who ended up paralyzed in a wheelchair. He was in a wreck traveling home after a weekend of skiing. He told me recently that his wheelchair does not define who he is. He travels all over the world motivating, inspiring, equipping and challenging people to not give up on life or themselves, but to become connected to a God who loves them and has a plan for their lives no matter how messed up things might seem. He refuses to blame anyone. He hasn't just reconciled with what has happened to him; he has learned to use it for a greater good. He continues to do the work he was always meant to do.

"People all around you are refusing to allow blame to keep them in the on deck circle just watching others play the game. They step up to the plate, problems and all, and give life their best shot. When asked the question, 'Is that where you want to stay?' they yell back, 'Hell no!' "

I told Poncho, "The choice to leave or stay on deck is yours. But keep this in mind: When you step up to the plate, you must accept responsibility for your actions from that moment on."

"I guess you're right, man," he said.

"You bet I'm right! I'm living proof!"

<u>THE RULES</u>

Rule No. 1:
Everything you do has consequences.

Rule No. 2:
If you want to be a winner, you can't go it alone.

Rule No. 3:
Life isn't fair.

Rule No. 4:
When you don't play by the rules, you can get hurt.

CHAPTER THREE

Accepting Responsibility

As I reflect on my time with Poncho, I realize that I gave him words when he had none. The following is the dialogue I imagined ran through Poncho's head as he reacted to me and to what we had shared so far. It was clear through his demeanor that he seldom talked about his feelings, pain or beliefs.

How can I tell this Sam dude that Poncho isn't my real name? I just threw that out in a flash — I didn't even think. But then again, how do I know his real name is Sam? Whatever. He seems real, but I don't know. I have to play it cool, you know? I don't want to tell him who I am. I have good street sense. I might be a little high, but I can still see someone fronting me a mile away. Still, my old lady tells me I trust people too much.

I have to hand it to him...the dude is stylin.' He looks like some kind of CEO type with that suit and that silver briefcase. But, then again he doesn't seem like the corporate type, and I don't think he's some government employee either. Maybe he's a businessman? I'm still trying to figure out his hustle. Working for an international organization that searches for what? Lost people? Could he be in organized crime? No, there's something about this guy that says he's the real deal, really legit. Oh well...

Me and my old lady, we've been having problems. We've been together for years. When I first met her, everything was great. But somewhere along the way things started going downhill. We started drinking, smoking, snorting. Not all at once, you know? It just sort of happened, and pretty soon we were arguing all the time. She just doesn't respect me as a man. She's always talking down to me, just like my mother used to do. What is it with women? They all sound the same.

I don't make a lot of money. I'm on disability and can't work much, and maybe that's why she doesn't respect me. But I can't help it that I got hurt on the job. And it's not my fault that I had to take stuff for the constant pain. That warehouse job really messed me up, you know?

But then, my old lady's got her own issues. Yeah, I promised to marry her a long time ago, but I just can't make myself do it. I'm sure she's angry about that. She's right, we've been together so long we might as well be married. But what's the big deal about getting married? We can't seem to have kids, so...? She blames herself for that part, and then turns around and blames me. I don't know. Now we're both unhappy, and both of us have this expensive drug habit. Seriously, though, I'm not an addict. I know I can stop if I want to.

I got my problems. I got my old lady to deal with. Then there's my past. My mother raised my brother and me alone; she did the best she could, but we never had much. I never knew my old man. I've been angry, really angry, about that. I guess this guy is right. The problems I got now are coming from all the bad stuff in the past. I might as well listen to what else he's got to say. I got nothing to lose.

"Man, you're right. I do need to stop blaming other people for my problems and get out of the 'on deck' circle."

Gradually, Poncho was becoming more engaged in our conversation. I quickly checked the train timetable to gauge how much time we had before reaching the next station.

"But you do understand, don't you, that giving up blame means accepting responsibility for your own actions? That's what the 'A' in BASES stands for: Accepting Responsibility. Let me tell you a story.

"Recently I was at a breakfast in Sacramento. It's called the California Prayer Breakfast. Each year, many of our political leaders gather for breakfast and prayer. A lot of young people attend, too. Maybe one year you could come with me. It's a real trip because there are people from all the political parties and religious groups at the breakfast. The one thing that joins them is the desire to pray for each other, for our state and our nation. We all need prayer."

"Me? Going to some fancy event like that? Naw, man, that's not my thing." Poncho dropped his eyes. I was beginning to sense his internal struggle, his low view of himself. I tried to be positive.

"Hey, it can be your thing. Don't count it out, OKAY? Anyway, the speaker this year was a U.S. senator. One of the things he said was, 'We can deal with each other irresponsibly, but we can't deal with each other inconsequentially.'"

"Uh...what did he mean by that?" Poncho asked.

"Well, he meant that our decisions and our actions have consequences. When we disobey our parents or our teachers, when we run a red light or go too fast around a curve, we may get away with it a time or two but eventually we will face consequences. As I sat there listening to the senator, I thought about the son of a good friend of mine who committed a crime. I don't know all the details, but the judge sentenced my friend's son to 16 years in the California Youth Authority. That's what they used to call the Division of Juvenile Justice."

"Aw, man, that's tough." Poncho said.

"Yeah, it was. The judge asked him if he had anything he'd like to say. After looking into the eyes of the people he had victimized and saying he was sorry for what he had done, he said, 'Your Honor, I've always known right from wrong, but today I'm learning about consequences.'"

"Uh, okay, I see what you mean. But how does that relate to your BASES thing?" Poncho asked.

"Sooner or later all of us need to leave the comfort of the on deck circle. Think of it like this: It's your turn to make decisions. You stand at the plate in the batter's position, waiting for the pitcher to throw the ball, preparing yourself to take the pitch. You take a few practice swings, and now you're ready. At least you think you're ready.

"You stare at the pitcher. You're worried. You feel a little nervous. You've always known that at some point you'd have to step up to the plate and face this pitch, regardless of whether it's a fast ball or a curve ball. It could be way outside, or it could come close enough to hit you. But it's your pitch. And it's here.

"The pitcher bends over at the waist and gets a signal from the catcher who's kneeling behind home plate. Again, he stares into your eyes, trying to sense whether you're afraid. Yeah, you're afraid. You hesitate. And just before he lets the ball go, you call 'time.'"

"Yeah, like when the batter steps back from the plate, knocks his cleats with the bat, adjust his gloves and shifts his helmet," Poncho reflected.

"You got it! That's it. And during this time out, you question whether you've got any chance of getting a hit. You wonder whether it's worth even trying when you'll probably fail."

The more we talked, the more often I found Poncho looking directly at me. I was gaining his trust little by little, and he continued to give me glimpses into his life.

Poncho responded, "That's kind of what I'm going through now, Sam. I had this great warehouse job. I was driving a forklift and I really liked it. One day I got out to check something and everything went wrong. Someone hadn't done their job – they didn't stack the boxes right. To make a long story short, I got injured on the job and now I'm on disability. I take pills for the pain, but it doesn't really help. So I started taking other things. Man, I need a break. I need a hit."

I appreciated his honesty. "Poncho," I said, "If you've decided to quit blaming someone else, you're well on the road to getting that hit you need. You've just got to accept responsibility and step up. Can I tell you another story?"

"Man, you're full of stories, aren't you?"

"Yeah, that's who I am. I'm a storyteller, just like my father."

"Okay, man, go ahead."

"When one of my nephews was in junior high school, he had to step up. He had lots of questions about the problems in his life. He wondered why he should be held responsible for his behavior. 'It's not my fault that my parents never got married,' he'd say. 'I didn't tell them to have me. They never showed any responsibility for what they did, so why should I?'"

"I can relate," said Poncho. "My mother didn't want me. She was always angry. She always talked down to me. Maybe she was angry with my dad – if you could even call him a dad. He was never around. It's like – why did they even have me? I didn't ask to be here, either."

"No, but you know what? None of us did. But the fact is, you are here, I'm here, we're all here. That's all that counts now. That's what I told my nephew. He didn't like hearing it. His eyes filled with tears and I could see his anger rising as he thought about all the hurt and pain, the disappointment and resentment. Probably a lot like what you're feeling right now, huh, Poncho?"

"Pretty much, yeah," he admitted.

"Well, my nephew's anger was rapidly turning to rage. He didn't want to hurt himself, but he felt like he had to hurt someone. After all, he was hurt and deserted by his father, so didn't he deserve to strike back? Fortunately, he didn't. Striking back wouldn't have helped him. In fact, he could easily have multiplied his own pain by inflicting it on others."

"I'm not into hurting nobody, Sam," Poncho confessed. "I guess I'm smart enough to know that isn't going to solve anything. I guess I just hurt myself instead."

"And that's bad, too. It's like stepping back into the batter's box, and when the pitch comes, deliberately throwing your body into the path of the ball!"

"Getting hit by a pitch. That hurts."

"You got that right. I've been there. Hard to believe that some people let themselves get injured on purpose. It's like they want to be put on injured reserve so they won't have to deal with the pressure of playing the game. Know what I mean?"

"Never thought of it that way."

"Poncho, as you walk to the plate, the stands are filled with spectators. Some are cheering you on and some are rooting against you. Some of them are even your family members. But you can't get to them and they can't get to you. There's no one to do this for you. You take the bat, squeeze it tightly and step back up to the plate. Over and over you say to yourself, 'I'll show them. I'm not like the rest. I'll accept responsibility for my actions. I'll use my anger constructively. I won't hurt others, and I won't hurt myself. But I need some help.'"

As we approached Suisun Station, I quickly did another mental survey of the information I still wanted to cover with Poncho. The train was making good time, and I wanted to have enough time to get all the way around the BASES.

"We're moving right along," I said, glancing back at my diagram. "I'm anxious to show you some ways to accept responsibility for your life. I'd even like to help you work through some of the painful events responsibly, and in a way that will allow you to look at yourself in the mirror and be proud of what you see. I want you to be able to reach out, help others, and make our world a better place because you were here."

"You're really concerned about me, aren't you?"

"Yes, I really am."

"Well, I appreciate that. Sam, how do you know when a person is living irresponsibly?"

"Hmmm… Good question. Let me see if I can help you discover the answer."

I gave another example. "A university student went to Planned Parenthood and was informed that the state had stopped funding HIV tests for college students. He went home and wrote a letter to his state senator to let him know how appalled he was at having to pay $25 for an HIV test, especially since AIDS is a life-threatening disease that is rapidly infecting the heterosexual population. He asked the senator to consider introducing a bill that would reinstate full coverage of the tests. What is your reaction, Poncho? Do you think this young man was responsible or irresponsible?

"I think he was being responsible," replied Poncho. "I mean, he was having himself checked out, wasn't he? Since HIV and AIDS is a social problem, I think it's the state's responsibility to pay for it. Right?"

"Poncho, Poncho, Poncho," I responded. I was grinning at him just a little. "To your credit, you just said you're going to stop blaming other people for things that happened to you. You've said you're going to accept responsibility. Now you're telling me you're going to let this guy off the hook?"

"I'm not sure I know what you mean, Sam."

"Okay, let me give you the definition of 'responsible' from the dictionary." I pulled out my pocket Oxford from my briefcase and started thumbing to the "R's." "Respond...response...responsible! Here it is. Can you read this for me, Poncho? The print is so small I can't see it without my glasses."

"Sure thing. Okay, it says, 'Responsible: Reliable, trustworthy, involving important duties.'" Poncho looked up at me. "Well, all right, maybe that doesn't describe this guy if he's worried about catching HIV. But still..."

I could tell that Poncho wanted to give the guy a break for even wanting to be tested.

"Maybe? Poncho, do you honestly think this guy cares about the women he's having 'casual' sex with? Do you think he cares about society's problems? Is the $25 the real issue? If he has time to have casual sex, doesn't he have time to get a part-time job to pay for the test? Then why doesn't he? Will the test results change his behavior? Is he being morally responsible? And will he ever answer for his behavior?"

Poncho was a little exasperated. "All these questions! All right, man, you tell me. What is the answer?"

"The senator wrote back and responded with another question," I said.

"Yeah well that sounds just like a politician, doesn't it?"

We both laughed. "I'll give you that one. But what this politician said made a lot of sense. He asked why a responsible single mother working to stay off welfare and take care of her children should have to help pay for this student's AIDS test so that he could continue to live irresponsibly! He told the young man to grow up and be responsible for his own actions!"

Poncho's expression betrayed his reaction even before he spoke. "Man, was that ever cold. He sounded like that Bob guy in that class you took while you were in prison."

"Oh, so you think the senator's reply was too harsh?"

"Yeah, a little. I can see where he's coming from, but—"

"Do you think he had the right to call the young man's behavior 'irresponsible?' "

"I guess so, since the kid was asking for a handout."

"And what about a total stranger telling a college student to 'grow up' and be responsible for his actions? Is that a stranger's role? Is it the role of a parent? A friend? Do you think this young man's desire to get an AIDS test was a sign of his being responsible?"

"Now that you put it that way, admitted Poncho, "I guess it isn't."

"Want to hear how the student responded to the senator's letter?" I asked.

"Sure."

"Well, the student wrote back accusing the senator of not caring about college students. He told the senator that he uses 'protection' every time he has sex. He claimed since AIDS was an epidemic, the tests need to be state-funded. He said he didn't appreciate being told to grow up and was sad to see such ignorance in our state government."

"Boy, he sure gave that senator an earful! But let me flip the script on you."

"Okay. Go ahead!" I replied.

"Don't you think that if someone is practicing 'safe sex,' uh, you know, using 'protection', they're actually being responsible?"

"What makes you think that condoms will protect you?"

"Well, that's what we hear in all the commercials and magazines. You're saying they don't work?"

There was no denying Poncho's interest in this topic, so I plowed on. "Poncho, I've worked with so many people who have gotten sidetracked and disconnected by being sexually irresponsible that I've done quite a bit of research into these questions. What the media does not tell you is that condoms fail one in six times among couples using them to prevent pregnancy or the spread of disease. Condoms break or slip off about 15 percent of the time."

"Say what?" he marveled, wide-eyed.

"That's what I said. More than one in ten uses fails! And condoms have a failure rate among teenagers of 20 percent. On average, if ten teens use condoms, two of them will be unprotected against disease or pregnancy. And one in five teen couples using condoms will become pregnant in one year!"

"I didn't know that."

"Yes, and condoms have similar failure rates for protection against STDs."

"You mean sexually transmitted diseases, right?"

"Right. And many of these diseases can't be cured. STDs can be unbelievably painful and embarrassing. They can prevent women from being able to have children. They can even be fatal."

"Yeah, I knew that part."

"Did you know that 2.5 million American teens contract a STD each year? 2.5 million! That's a lot of people! That's equivalent to the number of students who attend a California community college every year! That's 7,000 every day. What do you think? Pretty sad, wouldn't you say?"

"Yeah, I'd say so."

"So who is right – the senator or the student? Let me ask you this: is the student irresponsible if he has sex knowing that he could get AIDS? Is there anything he could do to protect himself other than using 'safe sex?' "

"Well sure, he could just not have sex, but—"

"Let me interrupt. Would it be too hard for a young man to save himself sexually until marriage? Is it possible to control sexual urges until you marry the one person you love enough to share your life with? Is that being unrealistic?"

"Yeah," answered Poncho. "I think it is. Besides, you can get AIDS other ways besides sex, right?"

"Yes, you're right. It's possible to get the disease from blood transfusions or from sharing dirty needles, but when you wait until marriage, you drastically reduce your chances of contracting the virus, and therefore you don't contribute to the spreading of the epidemic. That is living responsibly."

"But sex is a good thing, man."

"You bet it is. And within a marriage it's a beautiful thing."

"But Sam, what if you never get married? It's impossible to go through life and not have sex, especially for a man. A man has needs."

"Poncho, there are things you can't live without, like oxygen, food, water, sleep. But you can live without sex."

"Maybe so, but..."

I interrupted. "I know what's coming because I used to say the same things myself. A young man might think it's impossible not to have sex until marriage, especially if he's in an environment with a lot of pretty women around. But Poncho, you can do what you want to do."

" 'You can do what you want to do?' What does that mean?"

"I mean that you can do anything you really want to do. Just be honest and say, 'I *want* to have sex.' Don't lie to yourself and say, 'I have to have sex to live.' Do you remember A. C. Green, the basketball player who played with Magic Johnson and Kareem Abdul-Jabbar on the Lakers?"

"Sure do! Kobe Bryant is good, but that team with Magic, Kareem and Worthy— they were something!"

"Yeah, they were. But when all the other guys around him were doing their thing, A. C. Green abstained. The same goes for a friend of mine who's a freshman in college. And I know a guy who is almost 50, and he's a virgin."

"You gotta be kidding."

"Are they crazy, out of touch with reality, or have they chosen to live responsibly and treat women with respect?"

"I gotta hand it to them. They're strong men!"

"Yes they are, and as I said earlier, about 15 percent of condoms break. So is it responsible to take such a major risk for yourself and someone else, just to satisfy your sexual desires? Do you *have* to do what your physical urges suggest? Ask yourself,

'Am I accepting responsibility for my actions, or am I living irresponsibly?' AIDS is a problem we all have to face, from some perspective or another. This means that we must do whatever we can to find a cure. But until there is a cure, we must do all we can to stop the spread of the disease. One way to do that is by waiting until marriage to have sex. What do you think – is that too much to ask of you and your generation?

"It's asking a lot. I mean, you know, sex is everywhere."

"So is tobacco. People smoke, then they blame the tobacco companies when they get cancer. I had a relative who smoked, and it killed her. As her family, we've grieved her loss. We miss her. But we can't blame anyone else for her death. She made choices and she paid the consequences."

"I've had relatives who have died from smoking, too."

"So you know what I'm talking about. The whole thing about accepting responsibility is that our decisions have consequences. Life is more than a quick puff on a cigarette or a few minutes of pleasure. Sometimes, in order to be responsible, you must put aside what you want for the good of yourself, the people you love, and society in general.

"I've got to hand it to you, Sam, you're full of wisdom. I should have known by all that gray hair!"

"Hey, I like my salt and pepper hair, man!"

"Well, you do look distinguished!"

"Thanks," I chuckled. "Well let me wrap up this idea about accepting responsibility. Some people think there's nothing they can do about their problems. Their mom and dad never married, a single parent raised them, or they were molested, abandoned, or neglected. They might have even suffered in countless other ways."

"Yeah, like I said, some of that is me."

"But Poncho, some of that is me, too! Not having a father in your home makes a kid feel ashamed. I've been there. A child who is molested is damaged. I've been there, too. I was molested in juvenile hall."

"Aw, man, you were raped? And you admitted it?"

"Yes. If you can be honest with me about your past, I can be honest, too. And I can tell you that when it created a major disconnection between my wife and me, God helped me get beyond it.

"You see, Poncho, we all have pain in our past. Being abandoned and neglected is painful. Losing a parent when you're a kid is extremely painful. Having to bury a child, well, I can't find the words to describe the pain a parent must feel. When I was eight and my parents divorced, and there was nothing I could do to stop it from happening, but I could do something about how I responded to the pain I felt. Unfortunately, instead of finding help and talking it out, I acted it out in irresponsible ways and got myself in a lot of trouble. In the process, I hurt a lot of people who cared about me."

"Wow. You don't look like you've experienced all that."

"Well, I have. That's why I've said too many people, 'I'm one messed up person, and I come from a family with issues as well, we ALL do. "

Poncho stared right into my eyes. "Man," he said. "You may be messed up, but you're honest."

"When you're in my shoes, Poncho, you've got to be. I've stopped blaming others, and I've accepted responsibility for my actions. You can do the same – and you'll be ready to enter the game. You'll be on your way to first base sooner than you know, my friend."

"So what's the next letter?" Poncho asked. "We gotta get around the bases, right?"

"The next letter in the BASES acronym is "S" learning to Seek Help from others. That's so important in covering your bases. You ready for some more stories?"

"Sure. I got no place to go, and my old lady is somewhere else on this train."

CHAPTER FOUR

Seek Help

"Stumbling is not failing."
Malcolm X

The train was well on its way to Martinez. Poncho had been listening intently as I explained the principles of Banishing Blame and Accepting Responsibility for one's past, present, and future. We had already discussed the first two bases, but we had three more stops to go. We were on the first "S."

"The first 'S', " I explained, "stands for 'Seeking Help.' After you stop blaming others and can accept responsibility, you need to seek help. Hey, I've got another story for you."

"Well surprise, surprise," Poncho joked.

"My junior high years were a time in my life when I needed help. One of my teachers saw that. She asked me if I'd like to go with her and her husband to a college basketball game."

"Aw, man, you had the chance to go to a college basketball game?"

"Sure did. But I told her no. I still remember what Mrs. Maxwell said. She said, 'You know this school is in the playoffs, right? It should be a great game. We'd be honored if you'd go with us!'"

"Wow. She was practically begging you, huh? Did you end up going?"

"No, I just stared at her. I was thinking, 'Did this white lady really think I'd go to a game with her?' She had no idea of what kind of pain I was living with."

"The pain? What did that have to do with it? Going to a playoff game could have made you forget your pain, at least for a while!"

"Yeah, I guess so. But I thought they could never understand where I was coming from and what I was going through. I was this black kid from a family who didn't have a lot. I just knew that they appeared to be living the American dream. I figured they lived in a good house and drove nice cars. You know, I thought they were this perfect family, and besides, what would my friends say?"

"They'd probably have said you were selling out, right?"

"Right. And I had too much pride to accept a favor from her and then have to hear my friends be all over me for it. So when Mrs. Maxwell insisted, again I said, 'No thanks,' and walked away."

"Man, you were fronting. Tough on the outside, scared on the inside."

"You're absolutely right, Poncho. I was putting on the tough guy act. I wanted to go to that game big time. My friend's big brother played on the team! But like I said, I had too much p-r-i-d-e to walk into the gym with that white couple. I had some big problems, but I was refusing help."

"But Sam, sometimes pride is all we've got!"

"To a certain extent, pride is part of who you are. Take pride in your work, study habits, grades, personal hygiene etc. sure, that's fine. But Poncho, that's not the kind of pride I'm talking about. I was messed up, and rather than seek help, I let pride get in my way. I harbored anger for years. As a junior high student, it was starting to leak out. I couldn't hold it in any longer. My grades went down and I began to mess with drugs to cover up my pain. Instead of seeking help, I just continued with more and more negative behavior. This got me in a lot of trouble. I hope you won't let it happen to you."

"Sam, let me tell *you* a story."

"Okay, go ahead, man!"

"When I was in high school, a coach saw that I could really play baseball. Man, I could throw. I could catch. I could hit – and I was pretty fast running the bases, too. The guys I hung out with – they weren't athletic, at least not in baseball. Not that they weren't physical. They ran the streets. They robbed. They fought. You know, nothing really serious, just a lot of petty stuff. I didn't run with them, but I knew what they were up to."

"So what happened with your coach?"

"Man, was he persistent. He saw real talent in me and he kept pleading with me to try out for the team. He said, 'You are good enough to play college ball!'"

"Did you play?"

"No. I wanted to accept this coach's help, but I knew if I did, my friends would say I thought I was better than they were – because I wanted to better myself and get an education. I let a good opportunity slip away. Ever since then, I've always wondered where I'd be today if I had just listened to that coach."

"That's a legit question to ask yourself. But since you're here now, the right question to be asking is, 'What am I going to do with myself today?'"

"Yeah, I guess you're right."

"I needed help, too. I could have talked to a teacher, counselor, pastor, uncle, friend, older cousin – somebody. Anybody! You know what I'm saying? I could have kept on reaching out until I got the help I needed to overcome all the stuff I was dealing with. I didn't do that, and if you don't do that now, you'll live your entire life on first base. Ask someone for help and keep asking until you get the help you need and desire."

"Sometimes I think about asking people for help, like that coach. But my old lady – man, she thinks it's weak to ask for anything. Just like when I asked you for that paper."

"But that's wrong, Poncho. Asking for help is a way of showing strength. Refusing to ask for or accept help – now that's showing weakness."

"Man, I never looked at it like that. But try telling that to my old lady. That's probably why she was so angry at me."

"Could be. But that's her problem. Don't let it stop you from getting help when you need it. I wish someone had told me this stuff years ago. When I started college, I really needed help. I had no idea how to study."

"You went to college?"

"Yeah, I did. I didn't go right after high school, though. I got my high school diploma while I was locked up."

"Wow. You've come a long way. I can tell you're educated just by how you look and carry yourself."

"Thank you, and you know what? The same can happen to you. The reason I didn't know how to study is quite simple. When I was in high school I sat in the back of the class and played games. I didn't listen, and the only class notes I took were the ones handed to me from the girls."

"I heard that! You, a player?"

"Oh yeah, I was, but that was a long, long time ago, when I was young and dumb. I even got a girl pregnant. I was just 16. Now that, my friend, was being totally irresponsible. My son is still working through issues caused by my actions. But we're cool. He even named his first child after me. Let me tell you, I cried."

"Wow. I can see why."

"Anyway, in college it was different. By then I was married and had a family, so I didn't even think about writing notes to girls. I was determined not to mess up."

"You must have been really focused," said Poncho. "There are a lot of good looking babes in college."

"You got that right! But oh I wished I had paid attention in high school instead of goofing off and always being in trouble. I thought I was so cool back then, but in college I realized I was far from cool. In fact, I didn't know much at all. And I began to realize I needed help."

"So what did you do?"

"At first I had to accept responsibility for my own life – especially for my future, over which I was beginning to realize I had control. But I felt stuck on first base. I didn't know what to do. I knew I couldn't stay where I was, but I didn't know how to get to second base."

"So you asked for help, right?"

"Yes, I did. I started watching the people around me. I noticed three people in my classes – two guys and a lady. They took lots of notes, and they were getting good grades. I found out that they studied at the same times and places every day. They were disciplined. I was not. They sat in the front of the class. I sat in the back."

"So you hooked up with them?"

"Yes, eventually. But I hesitated. I knew I desperately needed help, and I knew they could probably help me, but *would* they? I was too afraid to ask. I thought, 'What if they say no? What if they reject me?' I wasn't sure I could handle their rejection. So for a while, I kept on trying to do the solo thing, but I kept failing."

"Man, college is hard, especially if you don't know what you're doing."

"It is. But if I can do it, so can you."

"So when did you get help?" Poncho asked.

"Halfway through the semester, can you believe it? I finally swallowed my pride and got up the nerve to talk to these students after class one day. I tried to be cool, you know what I'm saying? Even though it had been years since I refused to go to the game with Mrs. Maxwell, I still tried to be that same tough guy. Our conversation went something like this:

Me: 'Say, how you guys doing?'

Them: 'Great, Sam. What about you?'

Me: 'Oh, I'm cool. Everything's great.'

"Then one of them spoke up and said, 'Sam, we know you're new around here and like us, you're an older student. When we first came here, we all had trouble with our grades. We'd all been out of school for a while and weren't used to studying, but we've started helping each other out and we're finding our way. Anyway, if you ever need help, let us know. We'll help you like someone helped us. We'd be glad to include you.'"

I looked at Poncho. "Okay, so what would you have done?"

"I'd have taken them up on it. That's what I would have done."

"So did I. I stuttered and stammered, and finally choked it out that I could use some help. I told them I was having a little problem in math. Actually, I was having problems in all my classes."

"You were?" He seemed surprised.

"Poncho, I can't tell you what a struggle I was having in school. But approaching them was also a major struggle. Why? Because they were white.

It wasn't that there weren't any other blacks or Latinos in the school. But I was the only person of color in this class. And my life preservers were white. I almost let myself drown because of color."

"Yeah, I guess pride can weigh you down and make you sink."

"That's poetic, Poncho. And true. But you've got to go where the help is. Some people don't get help because they're stubborn. They refuse to go to someone of another culture or gender. All because of pride. In this case, I had to be willing to go where the help was: to the library, to the cafeteria, wherever these students hung out. But when I did, my grades went up. And believe me, that's the only direction they could have gone!"

We laughed, and then Poncho said, "You know, Sam, I'd like to go to college – maybe even one of the big universities one day."

"Well then you should try a community college first, just to get your feet wet."

"Yeah, I should check out Berkeley City College. That's the closest one to where I live. But who would I talk to?"

"Talk to someone in Admissions! Talk to a counselor! If money is an issue, talk to a Financial Aid Advisor! And when you talk to these people and they tell you things you don't want to hear, don't cop an attitude."

"What about my grades? They're not exactly anything I'm proud of."

"What about them? I didn't have good grades starting off. But when I got tired of failure, I got help.

When someone is willing to help you, accept it! Don't turn around and tell them they're wrong. That's like taking your car to a garage to be fixed. You tell the mechanic the problem. He looks at it and tells you the real problem is something else. You look at him, tell him he's nuts, and drive off. Remember: you brought your car to him!"

"I know what you're talking about. I know a lot about cars. I've worked as an auto mechanic on the side, just to make ends meet. My partners used to come to me about problems with their rides. When I told them what was wrong, they didn't believe me. It was like they disrespected me when I knew I could help them, or like they thought I didn't know what I was talking about."

"That's right. Accept help, even if you don't use it. You can always change your mind or do it your own way. But don't belittle what people offer you, especially when you reach out to them. I didn't use all the information my friends gave me, but I accepted it, and I made sure they knew I appreciated it.

"And getting help doesn't just apply to academic or intellectual challenges. That's just part of it. Some people have emotional, spiritual, and even physical problems. But they're unwilling to seek help from anyone. They may say, 'I don't have a problem. They do,' pointing to someone else. I did it myself, when my daughter Ericka was in college."

"You got a girl too, Sam?"

"Sure do. Some time ago my daughter told me that we were having trouble communicating and that we should go see a counselor."

"She told you that? Man, she's bold!"

"It's a good thing, too, but I told her I didn't have a problem and she wouldn't either if she'd just do what her father told her."

"I guess you put her in her place!"

"But Poncho, that was wrong of me. That was pride talking. My training in counseling should have taught me that, if nothing else!"

"You're a shrink?"

"No, I'm a counselor. Listen to me, Poncho. The person who says he or she doesn't have a problem usually does. That doesn't mean the other person doesn't. But claiming that someone else has a problem doesn't make yours go away."

"So what did you do?"

"I swallowed my pride, and we went to see a counselor."

"You took your daughter's advice?"

"Yep. I fought it all the way, I was glad we went because our relationship improved. But it never would have happened if Ericka had not been seeking help. She didn't have to do that. She could have gone on blaming me. She might have said, 'Hey, it's on you, Daddy. You're the parent.' But even as a teenager, she showed more maturity in this situation than I did. I really love her for what she did.

"The scary thing is that some people look for help in the wrong places. Some believe suicide is all the help they need."

"I've thought about suicide before," Poncho confessed, "but I just couldn't bring myself to do it. I love life too much, I guess. And even though we have problems and my old lady really gets under my skin at times, I love her. I wouldn't want to leave her like that."

"Thinking about suicide is something that many of us do. But you're right, life is precious, and if we killed ourselves, we'd be hurting the people we love and those who love us as well.

"After my stepmother died, my father was so distraught that some people thought he wanted to kill himself. We were driving around one day when my father said to me, 'Sam, I'm going to tell you something, and I'm only going to say it once. If you ever find my body and there's a suicide note, check the handwriting. It ain't mine. Life is short enough, and I don't plan to make it any shorter.'

"When a person is totally disconnected or separated from themselves, from family, friends, the community and God, what is there to live for? Later on in my life, I became disconnected as well. Because of my alcohol problem, I went to Alcoholics Anonymous. There I found help and some very important principles. They gave me the tools to overcome my addiction and start changing my behavior."

"Man, I've had a drinking problem for years, and yeah, like I said before, I've done a little drugs, but nothing hard core."

"Poncho, to be honest with you, it sounds to me like you're in denial."

"Oh yeah?"

"Yep, sure does. Let me continue to answer your question. At first I hated A.A. People would actually stand up and say, 'Hello, my name is...' They'd say their first name only, and then they'd say, '...and I'm an alcoholic.'"

"Yeah, I've heard that before. Sounds pretty corny."

"It does, but they have you say that for a reason. They want you to be honest with yourself. I didn't think I was an alcoholic. I was in denial. In fact, I wasn't sure I had a problem with alcohol at all, when the problem was that I couldn't get enough of it. I acted crazy when I drank it; I got depressed when I couldn't. But I didn't have a problem. I thought A.A. couldn't help me."

"So you left?"

"I sure did. I still acknowledged I had a substance abuse problem, and to my credit, I sought help elsewhere."

"Where did you go? Oh wait, I know – N.A."

"Right. Narcotics Anonymous – more of the same. There, too, a person would stand up and say his first name, followed by, 'I'm a drug addict.' I left that meeting."

"So where did that leave you?"

"Well, I tried church. The difference there was that they were confessing they were all sinners and needed God's help. I wasn't going to admit or confess anything. *I didn't need help.*"

"Sounds like you were in denial, too Sam," grinned Poncho.

"I sure was! Then one day I discovered just why I hated these groups. It was their honesty! I wasn't ready to be honest about much of anything. I was still blaming everyone else. I wasn't ready to accept full responsibility for my actions. I wanted everyone else to change. Then I wouldn't have to. I didn't seek help because I had convinced myself I didn't need the help, but one day I broke down, admitted who I was and what was going on inside of me, and I asked a friend for help. Seeking help is vitally important to making it in life.

I returned to the baseball diamond I drew on the paper. We were about to reach the third base. I recapped with Poncho. "We've talked about being lost, feeling disconnected and the importance of forming positive connections. You've got to admit you need help, and accept it when and where it's offered. Don't refuse help because of your hang-ups or your pride, but refuse the wrong kind of help— like the easy way out or listening to people whose 'help' only brings you down.

"So what's the next base?"

"The next base is 'E', Envision Success! You need to be able to close your eyes and see what it's going to look like when you get where you want to be. You've got to see it before you see it!"

"Uh, what?"

"Let's take a look"

CHAPTER FIVE

Envision Success

"I skate to where the puck is going to be,
not where it's been."
– Wayne Gretsky

A man who stands for nothing will fall
for anything."

I'm hoping Poncho is thinking, "*Envision Success.
Ok, Sam says I need to envision my success. That's
probably what I need to do, but it just seems so...
so difficult. I can't envision my success. I really can't.
My life seems hopeless right now.*

*Sometimes it feels as if my life is like the inside
of a barrel. I have a ladder and it's my only way out,
so I start climbing, but then I slip and fall back down
to the bottom. I try to get back on the ladder, but
other people get in my way. They get ahead of me
and I struggle with them, all of us trying to get on*

the same ladder. Finally I'm back on the ladder and then someone ahead of me steps on my hands. I lose my grip and end up at the bottom again. For years I've been in this cycle of climbing and struggling and falling and climbing and struggling and falling. Now this man wants me to "envision success" by climbing and struggling some more?

But he's right. I know the dude is right. There's got to be more to life than what I've had so far. I'm not happy. I'm disgusted with myself – with the drinking, the smoking, the snorting— all of it just to cope. I hate arguing and always having to defend myself to my old lady. But in spite of all the bad breaks I've had, I know I can do better. I want to do better.

There was a time when I did do better. I did pretty well in high school. I think the coach envisioned my success. He saw something in me, and it was more than just my baseball talent. He took an interest in me; he was kinda like a father. He invited me to some youth program at his church. He wouldn't let up on me, so I finally went. I don't even remember the name of the place, but it really surprised me. I felt good being there. I felt at peace. I felt accepted. I've got to admit it: I felt loved there. I was beginning to feel good about myself. But I didn't tell my friends. I kept to myself, sneaking trips to this church like it was something bad! They found out anyway, and when they did, where was hell to pay. They ragged on me and wouldn't stop. I couldn't deal with it. I know, I shouldn't have let it get to me but I did. I quit going to church. To this day, I regret it.

I know what Sam's talking about. I'm in so deep that it's going to take years to climb out. But I know I can do it if I just try. I want to be a man and stop blaming others for all my faults. I need to accept responsibility for being in this barrel in the first place. I need to get some help if I want to get out. Maybe getting help could help me get to the place where I could envision my success..."

I interrupted his thoughts. "Say, Poncho. We're almost at Emeryville. Want me to go on?"

"Yeah, man, go ahead. Please."

"You know, lots of people choose to stay on second base. They believe they've made enough progress so that they don't feel like failures. To others, they seem successful, and for a brief moment, they feel successful. But there's a problem."

"A problem?"

"Yes. The problem is that they don't *see* themselves as a success. Failure is so much a part of them that they can't see past it."

"How do you know what they're seeing, Sam?"

"Because their actions speak so loudly you can't hear what they're saying."

"I guess that's me. I feel like a failure. My friends may think I'm cool, but inside it's different."

"And that's what I'm saying. Our actions may fool other people, but we can't fool ourselves. You can't envision success if you don't have a mental picture of yourself being a success."

"So it's an attitude thing?"

"Yes, and many times that attitude shows in how we react to others. Let me give you an example of something I noticed with you. Remember when we rolled into the Davis Station, and all of those UC Davis students came aboard?"

"Yeah, what about it?"

"You changed."

Poncho looked puzzled. "I did? How so?"

"Here were all these kids toting backpacks, laptops, and blasting tunes on their iPods. And all of a sudden, your body language changed."

"I didn't notice it."

"But I did. When those college kids came around, you put on this street thing, showing them that you were cooler, tougher than they are."

"Yeah, maybe. Probably so, now that I think about it. You gotta be that way to survive on the street, man."

"I know. I've been there. But your behavior towards them was a lot different than the way you interacted with me."

"Well," Poncho laughed, "I ran into you! I was just trying to be respectful."

"Yeah, and to your credit, you were. With me, another adult who's a little older, you acted one way. But to young people, you projected yourself differently, based on how you envisioned yourself."

"Well I felt good being around you. My guard was down. I didn't feel threatened. A little skeptical, maybe, but not threatened. But those kids are close to my age. It feels different."

"I know what you mean. You're looking at a guy who was locked up for five years, remember? You've just illustrated my point: with those kids, you envisioned yourself differently, and it affected how you acted. Do you see what I'm saying?"

"I think so."

I went on. "In my opinion, the wisest man ever to live was King Solomon. Here's what he had to say about envisioning your success: 'For as a man thinks within himself, so is he.' That's what I'm talking about. It is what you think of yourself that truly determines whether you will be a failure or a success."

"I see that. It's all on the inside."

"That's right. It's not me, not your girlfriend or your mother, not a teacher, not your friends, not even your absent father. The person with the most power to determine your future is you."

"So what do I do to change the way I see myself?"

"I'm glad you asked the question, Bishop Cleaveland, an old black preacher, once said, 'If you don't see it *before* you see it, you ain't never gonna see it.'"

"See what?"

"Well, Poncho, he would take two fingers and tap his temples— like this." I demonstrated by tapping my temples with my fingers to indicate my mind. "He took those same two fingers and pointed to his eyes, then he would point straight forward, referring to what you actually see with your eyes. I think you get the point."

"Yeah, I do."

"And so did Dr. M. Norvel Young. He was president and chancellor of Pepperdine University. We became friends when we served on a board together."

"Pepperdine? Where's that?"

"Pepperdine is now in Malibu, California, overlooking the Pacific Ocean, but back in the day it was located in South Central Los Angeles. One day Dr. Young took a friend for a ride out on the coast to look at a potential site for the new college. He stopped his car, looked at the sagebrush-covered hills, and said, 'This is the site where I want to build our new campus.' His friend, thinking he must be joking, said, 'Who's going to attend? Billy goats?' He had not seen what Dr. Young saw, but very soon, he did."

"Was this dude successful?"

"He sure was. The campus is breathtaking. It sits on the very site he saw that day, overlooking the blue Pacific. It has a huge gymnasium, grassy playing fields, and an Olympic size swimming pool. 'ABC Wide World of Sports' filmed events at this pool for years. Man, Poncho, it's gorgeous. I wish you could see it."

"How did they build it?"

"Well before any land was cleared or foundation laid, Dr. Young and others drew up plans. Those plans let others see on paper how the campus would look."

"So someone just had to think all that up?"

"That's the point, Poncho. Someone had to think of it. The plans came to life in Dr. Young's mind. He visualized the school before they put the first drawings on paper, before a single building was constructed."

"I'd call that envisioning success!"

"Exactly. Envisioning success. He saw it before he saw it, and now we all see it. Remember I told you how difficult it was for me to go to school? When I started college, it was tough. I could read, but not at college level."

"I'm not really a great reader either. The words don't always make sense to me."

"Well there are programs and tutors who can help you in college. My grades were very poor until I met those three students I mentioned. When I finished my first year I was very happy, but I didn't think I could finish three more years."

"Oh. You would have stayed right on second base, then. You didn't know if you could push yourself any more?"

"You got that right. I needed to be motivated and inspired."

"That coach I told you about, the one who thought I was really good, he would have pushed you."

"Sounds like it! Anyway, someone invited me to the graduation ceremony that year. I didn't really want to go, but I did. I sat in the stands with all the families and friends."

"The only other graduation I ever went to was my baby sister's high school graduation."

"Do you remember how excited you were?"

"Oh man, do I!"

"Well it's even more exciting at a college graduation – the music, the caps and gowns, the anticipation, the mixture of pride and relief on the faces of the students and their families. There's nothing like it. At the ceremony, they called each student's name in alphabetical order. As they walked across the platform, they shook hands with the president, received their diplomas, posed for a picture, and returned to their seats."

Poncho continued reminiscing. "We had a large senior class the year I graduated. My name was at the end of the alphabet, so it seemed to take forever to get to me."

I laughed. "Yes, sometimes, especially for large schools, it takes a very long time. But everyone wants to be recognized. At this graduation, when they got to the H's my mind began to wander. Then they called out a name where mine would have been had I been in that graduating class. Poncho, I closed my eyes, and I saw—" I paused for a moment.

"Saw what?"

"I saw my parents sitting in the stands, crying and smiling with pride. I saw my grandmother with tears streaming down her cheeks. I saw my sons and daughter. I saw my friends. Then *I saw me.* I was wearing a cap and gown. I walked across the platform, shook the president's hand and took hold of my diploma. Then I opened my eyes."

"Envisioning success," remarked Poncho.

"That's right. I had three years to go, but I had *seen* my graduation. That's what I mean when I say, 'envision success.' It's what Bishop Cleveland meant when he said, 'If you don't see it before you see it, you ain't never gonna see it.' It's what Dr. Young saw before the first spade of soil was turned at Pepperdine's new campus. It's what King Solomon meant when he said, 'For as a man thinks within himself, so is he.' It's what motivates some people to move beyond second base. Henry Ford, the car inventor, said it too – "Whether you believe you can or cannot, you are absolutely right!" Victor Frankl, a writer and philosopher, survived the Holocaust and the horrific torture of his friends and family. He says in his book, *Man's Search for Meaning*, that his survival was anchored by the vision he had seeing himself teach about the Holocaust. Those visions helped him survive, and he did teach after the war. He became a significant leader and writer in the name of peace and humankind equity.

"Poncho, ever heard of Helen Keller?"

"The name sounds familiar. Wasn't she that blind lady?"

"She wasn't just blind. She couldn't hear, and she couldn't talk, either. She was once asked if there was anything worse than being blind, to which she answered, 'It is a terrible thing to see and have no vision.'"

"Man, I like that. That's deep," Poncho reflected.

"Yeah, it is. And if you want to move from second base to third, you must keep a clear vision of where you're going. That day at the college graduation, I gained a vision. From that day on, I knew I'd graduate. It was tough, very tough. There were many distractions. I wanted to quit many times, but I didn't. I had already envisioned my success and knew I was going to make it a reality. What I saw motivated me."

"Sam, are there times when someone gets that vision and still doesn't make it?"

"Sadly, yes. Some folks become victims to what I call the 'vision stealers.' As I see it, there are four major vision stealers. *Parents can be vision stealers* when they tell their kids, 'You're stupid,' or 'You're going to grow up to be just like your no-good father.'"

"My mother – she told me that."

"Well your mother, God bless her, was instrumental in stealing your future by planting negative seeds. Many people end up living their lives on second base, unable to see their way to third base because of something some adult said when they were kids. They just can't shake their minds free from those ugly words."

"What are the other vision stealers?"

"It's a shame, but your *friends can be big vision stealers* as well. Friends can be the most powerful vision stealers of all; even more so, at times, than parents."

Poncho commented, "Probably because we hang out with our friends more."

"You got it right. We give them the ability and the right to steal our vision because we want to keep our friends happy; too often we give things up to stay with our friends. People often fear the unknown and would rather stay with what is familiar. For many people, friends are their most important assets, and they protect them at all costs. They even protect them when it means giving away their futures to stay in the now.

"The third *vision stealers are unexpected events*. The death of a parent, being molested, a wreck that leaves you paralyzed (like my friend Gary), getting hooked on something that distracts you, all these things can get you lost and eventually disconnect you from life and your purpose or your vision.

"And the fourth is *anything else that comes into your mind that sends negative messages about your vision.* The books you read, the music you listen to, the TV shows and movies you watch can all become vision stealers."

"Why? I mean, how?"

"They deliver messages telling you who you are or should be. You may not believe them at first, but if you listen and read long enough, you will. You'll begin to act just like what you read. You'll act like the music you listen to or like the characters you see on TV. Those words turn into pictures in your head, and the pictures turn into actions; your actions determine your future."

"It's like a chain reaction."

"It sure is. Do you remember Arsenio Hall?"

"Yeah, I remember that dude. He was the one that always used to say, 'Things that make you go, hmmmm...'"

"That's him. When Arsenio Hall was a kid, he wanted to grow up and be like Johnny Carson."

"The King of late night TV talk shows! Where did he get that idea?"

"From Johnny Carson. But do you think Johnny ever visited his house?"

Poncho laughed. "I doubt it! I can see where you're going with this though. If we're influenced by watching TV, Arsenio's idea probably came from watching Johnny Carson, huh?"

"That's exactly right. Arsenio Hall began to see himself in Carson's chair, hosting guests, asking questions and making jokes, laughing with his audience."

"He probably didn't envision as a child saying, 'Things that make you go, hmmmm...'"

"Yeah, Poncho, he probably didn't think of that until he got his show. But when he was a kid, he envisioned his success. Can you think of any other examples where people envisioned success?"

"Sure. Look right over there at The Rock."

"You mean Alcatraz?"

"Hey, someone had to envision building a prison on that island."

"You're right," I said. "As a matter of fact, it was an Army fort before it was a prison. Somebody had to envision that as well!"

"And look, there's another one right here in the Bay."

"I know where you're going – The Golden Gate Bridge!"

"Yeah, that's it."

"Sometimes," I told Poncho, "we need to grab hold of what others see in us. In prison, I chose to believe what my parents saw in me and not what others were saying. When I first got out of prison, I was so messed up there's no way I'd have ever seen myself as Dr. Samuel Huddleston. But my wife saw it and began telling me, 'Sam, you ought to go back to school and earn your doctorate.' I thought she was nuts. I was an ex-felon with only a high school diploma that I got in prison. But I chose to believe her words and I started taking the first classes."

"Wow. Dr. Samuel Huddleston. Now that's what I'm talking about!"

I realized that we didn't have enough time to make it all the way home, so I gave Poncho my business card and told him we'd have to hook up later and finish.

"Thanks, man. I gotta hand it to you, Sam. You got it goin' on."

"Thank you, Poncho. So, what do you think?"

"Oh, about what you said, envisioning success? It just seems so...beyond me, man. My old lady is not like your wife."

Poncho became pensive. I imagined he might be thinking, "*Envision Success. Okay, Sam says I need to envision my success. That's probably what I need to do, but it just seems so … so difficult. I can't envision my success because people like me don't get the chances. Wait a minute – now I'm blaming other people. I just can't see myself being the up-and-coming dude, not now, I really can't. My life seems hopeless and it is my fault. I am not even worth all this talk. What's up with this dude? Does he think I am one of the lost people he is trying to find? All I did was get on this train with my old lady. I didn't expect all this … I need to get away from this dude. He's making me sound crazy. Damn, I did it again – he isn't making me do anything. Now I am crazy in the head with these voices.*

"Sam, I was just thinking. I got so much bad stuff in my life. It's like it haunts me. Sometimes I can't see anything past today, and for sure I don't expect anything good."

"Well Poncho, when you get to this 'envision success' stage of the game, you can—"

Poncho cut me off abruptly. "Sam, I was just thinking about my life. There are some things really holding me back, you know what I mean? I just don't see myself ever getting out of the cycle of climbing and struggling and falling."

"Ok. Be honest with me. What is this struggling and falling all about?"

A few moments of uncomfortable silence followed. Finally Poncho spoke.

"All right. I'll be honest. It's the smoking weed and snorting coke. I even have some on me now."

"Look, Poncho, there is a way out! I've been there! I've done that! Man, I've been where you are!"

"Yeah, you said you were into all that, back in the day."

"I was and I got out of it! I got tired of the life. I got tired of the ups and the downs. I got tired of getting high, feeling good for a while, then crashing, craving more, and robbing and stealing from folks just to get the stuff. I got tired of sleeping with one eye open. I got tired of the excitement of getting that weed, or whatever, just to get high. And it doesn't really satisfy, does it? Then the process starts all over again!"

"Yeah. That's what I'm going through now."

"I know, I know. Many people get stuck right here. They don't realize that change is so demanding. They get tired and they get tired of being tired. Asking for help isn't easy. Pride can be a dangerous flaw."

Poncho grew angry. "I'm asking you, man, I'm asking! What can you do for my life? Are you going to give me a job? Introduce me to your daughter?"

"I can understand your anger, Poncho. Anger is an easy way to walk away from your life. But I also see your sincerity. I can see the pain and the hope in your eyes, and I'm here to help you. I have given you some basics, you can go on from here or go back to where you have been." Poncho, the real question is, what are you going to do with this new information?

My friend I can tell you this, change for me began one lonely night when I looked into the heavens and told god I did not believe he existed, but if he did exist, I was a candidate for whatever he had to offer. Poncho, my life has never been the same since that night. You might want to start with that simple, God I don't even believe you exist prayer.

He smiled as if to say, I just might, I just might.

The train was slowing to a stop, and I knew our time was at an end. I began gathering my things. Poncho spoke up. "Sam, I've got to go, man. Can I have that piece of paper with the baseball diamond and all BASES stuff on it?"

"Of course," I replied. "Here, take my pen, too."

"Your pen? You're serious, man? That's a nice pen!"

"That's right. It's yours."

"Wow. Thanks. And thanks for everything, man. I'll catch you later."

"Call me. I will be ready when you and the voices in your head say it is time."

"How did you know about the voices?"

"Everyone has them; it's part of how we resolve problems. We talk to ourselves. When you don't like the answers you are getting, try talking to God instead of just dialoging with yourself. Talking to God is the first step in prayer, and everyone who prays gets answers." That's where I started, talking with God and being honest with myself.

Poncho just looked at me. It was as if he finally got what I meant when I said I work for an organization that finds lost people. He said, "You think I am one of the lost people don't you."

I answered simply, "Yes." It was like he just got the punch line of a joke.

"You do GOD for a living and that's how you got to buy those clothes and those shoes? Working for GOD?"

"Yes."

"I just got found, didn't I?"

"It seems so Poncho. You have some decisions to make. Take the bases one at a time. Remember, it's never too late to run the BASES and change your life."

"Thanks, Sam."

"Your welcome, Poncho." I watched him walk off. I wondered if he would use the pen and the phone numbers. I prayed for him to find his way, and I hoped that our time together would reconnect Poncho with himself and God, and direct him to the future he deserved and desired. I hoped the BASES would help change his life as they had changed mine.

CHAPTER SIX

A Step-by-Step Plan

The principles I shared with Poncho dealt mainly with attitudes. Negative attitudes often consume people to the point that they live their lives blaming others, refusing to accept responsibility for their actions, and resenting help. Optimists, on the other hand, view life in terms of new and positive opportunities; they envision their success and the pathways they must take to get there.

There's no way to get where you want to go until you are willing to implement the proper strategies for getting there. To do that, you've got to develop a Step-by-Step Plan. The plan must include preparation for the roadblocks along the way because "vision stealers" can trip you up and distract you. They'll attempt to dampen your enthusiasm or try to convince you that your goal isn't important.

Choosing the right friends to surround us is the <u>first</u> step in developing a plan. I cannot emphasize

enough the importance of building wise friend-
ships. Those we allow into our private world need
to be what motivational speaker and author Les
Brown labels "OQP" – Only Qualified People. Your
friends should have your best interests at heart and
be invested in your success. They should champion
the work it takes you to reach your goals. The best
"qualified people" will help with your plans – they
can show you what you cannot envision because of
your blind spots, but beware of "vision stealers," or
people who have no plans who don't want to see
you succeed in yours. They are everywhere, and
they *will* steal your dreams if you let them, but they
must be given permission to steal your dreams.
People like this view life and themselves in a negative, self-defeating way, and they'll do all they can to
make sure you're defeated, too.

<u>Next</u> you must develop a working plan. Though
it's never too late to develop and begin working a
plan, it's also never too early. Much heartache could
be avoided if, even as children, we are guided into
the process of formulating step-by-step plans for our
futures. A few years ago, I heard a speaker present
this truth:

A DREAM + A PLAN + ACTION = REALITY
A DREAM – A PLAN – ACTION = A DREAM.

When creating a working plan, you've got to ask
yourself, "What is my dream or vision for myself?"
Sometimes, this actually boils down to considering
questions like, "What do I like doing? What fulfills

me? What comes naturally to me? What are some things I currently excel at?" List your answers. Playing a sport, writing poetry, singing, playing chess, making others laugh, excelling in math or science, swimming, rapping, cooking – all of these can give you clues to your purpose in life. I met a man whose job was to taste ice cream. He loved to eat, and he made a life from that love!

The <u>third</u> step to take is to really listen to the positive things others say about you. When people say things like, "Boy, you write so well," or "You sure have a gift for working with people," heed those compliments! You may discover strengths you hadn't considered until someone else sees them first. I tell my grandchildren that they don't have to know exactly what they want to be when they grow up, but I encourage them to ask themselves these same questions and listen to what others say about their natural abilities. These valuable clues will help them discover their eventual life paths.

<u>Fourth</u>, your plan should include finding someone who is already doing what it is you hope to do, and watch that person closely. Ask him or her how they arrived where they are and what obstacles got in the way. Write down their answers, and be willing to learn. Ask to be mentored, and set aside time for whatever your role model will devote to teaching you. Be willing to take direction; don't ask for feedback that you are not open to accepting. Mentors should be critical friends that will tell you the truth and invest in your success by challenging you to be better.

Pick your guides and mentors carefully. Make sure they live their lives in a manner that you want to emulate. Make sure the plans you create don't ask you to lie, cheat or manipulate. Lying, cheating and manipulating may help you gain access to certain situations, but they never sustain you. Lives built on tenuous or shaky foundations always fail eventually.

And remember, as you create the steps in your plan, don't lose sight of the goal. Start by setting small goals that you can reach easily, and then build to the harder ones, but don't focus so much on each step that you lose sight of what you've envisioned.

My son Andre taught me how to realize a goal and become successful. He was a good basketball player in high school, but he wasn't satisfied with just being good. He wanted to be even better, so he formulated a step-by-step plan of action. The following five steps are the tools I learned watching and being a part of my son's game plan.

First, *seek advice* from the one who knows best. During the summer before his senior year, he went to the coach and asked, "What do I need to do to be a better player?" And the coach told him things that, if implemented, would improve his game.

Second, *make a list outlining what needs to be done.* He didn't try to memorize them. He knew that the palest ink is better than the most retentive memory. A list can always be thrown away once it's not needed, but if you forget it, it's gone.

Third, *look at this list daily.* He put the coach's comments on the wall beside his bed. Each morning and evening he reviewed them. They were the first and last things he saw daily. He even slept with his basketball!

Fourth, *practice and get feedback and practice some more*. Every day during the summer, Andre worked out at the local middle school. I knew where to find him if I needed him. If he couldn't get to the school, he practiced in front of the house. The point is that he practiced every single day. Practice may not always make perfect, but perfect practice does.

Finally, experience the success and make it a memory. For Andre, it all came together in the first game of the year. He scored almost 30 points. That's what can happen when you practice every day, and that's how you get from third base to home. You follow a plan. You can dream, hope, and desire all you want, but without a plan you'll never get off third base. Remember:

A DREAM + A PLAN + ACTION = REALITY
BUT
A DREAM − A PLAN − ACTION = A DREAM

There is nothing sacred or magical about the BASES method of describing the path to success. I happen to love baseball, but I might have used an acronym from football or business or medicine to name these principles, and yet, my many years of counseling people, young and old, rich and poor, uneducated or educated, have taught me that these basic principles can't be ignored. Until you learn to stop blaming others and accept responsibility for your own life, seek and accept help from those who have walked before you, and believe in your own success and develop a plan to get there, you will be left behind. It is your choice.

Your decision today to step out of the dugout and onto the field can be the beginning of an exhilarating run, one that will someday see you coaching others in the very principles that have led you to a fulfilling, satisfying life.

More of what others are saying about Grand Slam...

"Dr. Huddleston is a man of faith and wisdom that talks the talk and walks the walk. Every single and precious suggestion to help another person looking for inner peace is delivered with humility and a deep understanding of our frail human condition".
-Peppino D'Agostino, Internationally known professional guitarist

Sam's presence as a man on a mission is felt the minute you meet him... Without Pastor Sam in my life I am not sure if I would today be clean and sober. I probably would not have started and stuck with the Reach Out program that has changed so many lives. My faith and love for the Lord would not be where it is today. Words and love are what I have to thank the man who I believe saved and gave me life.

Dr. Huddleston will always be a leader and a great teacher and I know that his new book will change lives around the world.
-Earl Miller, CAADAC II, Certified drug and alcohol counselor and educator

Your book was awesome and inspiring . . . it was a train ride full of wisdom sharing!! I can see it being used in our high school Alternative School setting in a class all students take called Life Skills. Every year the instructor chooses a book to read with the class and "Grand Slam" would be perfect to encourage those students at this stage of their life when so many of their decisions are based on "wrong-thinking". How amazing would it be that each of them learn the strategies/concepts of BASES and use it!!
-Miss Norma González, 10th/12 grade counselor, Othello High School, Washington

I have over 25 years of work experience dealing with Juvenile delinquents in the Criminal Justice System. In my past experiences one of the key components missing in these young adult lives is structure. *Grand Slam* will help give young and old adults a powerful tool.
-Charles E. Sanders, Retired Juvenile Detention Manager and Counselor, Palmetto, FL

Dr Sam Huddleston is truly a gift to humanity. He has an acute sense of insight into human development and sees the potential in people that society has over

looked or marginalized. He is a great inspiration, a true friend, and I call him my big brother.
-Senior Pastor Alfonso Schilder, Mount Hope Worship Centre, Cape Town, South Africa

I have had the privilege of seeing Sam Huddleston present the principles in this book to individuals in church, school and prison. I have personally witnessed the impact that the principles have had on my family and many others. If you apply the strategies to your life, you can go from a "strike out" to a "home run".
-Greg Cambell, Ph.D. Candidate, Walden University, Leadership and Organizational Change Specialization, Chief Deputy Inspector, U.S. Postal Inspection Service

My dear friend, Dr. Sam Huddleston, has written this book for people with a "troubled soul". Which one of us hasn't experienced times when we have been deeply troubled: at home, on the job, or just in the course of daily life?

Sam has experienced more than most of us. To his credit, he has taken the tougher road. Through his amazing life, from prison to leader in one of the largest churches in America, Sam has learned the principles necessary to achieve victory over the troubled soul. In this book he gives us a step-by-step method to achieve it.
-Tim Leslie, Retired California state senator

I know Sam. I know his wife, I know his children, and I know his grandchildren.

When you meet his grandchildren you would never know the terrible past that Sam has escaped from. These amazing grandchildren are the #1 evidence that what Sam writes about in "Grand Slam" actually works.
-Pastor Steve Madsen, Cornerstone Fellowship, Livermore, CA

Whether from the East or from the West, everyone can identify with these issues. This book will be a real blessing to many.
-Rev. Fermin Bercero Ed.D., President, Bethel Bible College, Manila, Philippines

For those who have reached a place where they see no hope, Sam offers a tool, a link to moving forward and finding the fulfillment and wholeness that God has intended for all who believe.
-Dr. Sharon L. Anderson, Professor, Bethany University, Santa Cruz, California

Until one can actually remove the shield and become extremely honest about his or her own pain, sorrow, and hopelessness, healing cannot occur. It's all about admitting it and facing it...and that's what *Grand Slam* will teach you to do.
-John Withers, Marriage and Family Therapist

Works Cited

Alcoholics Anonymous, Fourth Edition, 2001, published as "anonymous", but really written by William G. Wilson, Henry Parkhurst, Joe Walsh, and many other people.

Alcoholics Anonymous World Services, Inc. New York, NY, 2001.

Ashe, Arthur and Arnold Rampersad. *Days of Grace*: A Memoir. New York: Alfred A. Knopf 1993

Les Brown. *Live Your Dreams*, New York, Avon Books, 1992.

Carroll, Lewis. (English author Charles Lutwidge Dodgson). *Alice Adventures in Wonderland* (1865).

Chass, Murray. "Umpire Dies After Collapsing on Field, "*The New York Times,* April 2, 1996.

"Helen Keller." BrainyQuote.com. Xplore Inc, 2010. 12 May. 2010. http://www.brainyquote.com/quotes/authors/h/helen_keller.html

Norman King. Arsenio Hall. New York: William Morrow and Company. 1993.

ThinkExist.com Quotations. "Johann Wolfgang von Goethe quotes". ThinkExist.com Quotations Online 1 Apr. 2010. 12 May. 2010 http://einstein/quotes/johann_wolfgang_von_goethe/

To contact Sam Huddleston,
write him at:
P.O. Box 995
Benicia, CA 94510

Or visit his Web site: www.samhuddleston.com

Other books written by Sam Huddleston
Five Years to Life:
The story of a wayward son and his father's
relentless love.
Onward Books, 2007

Breinigsville, PA USA
21 July 2010
242155BV00001B/2/P